MW00936130

# Free Pass: The Demise of Accountability

## M. Randall Long

ISBN 13: 978-1542466172
ISBN-10: 1542466172

Copyright November, 2016 - M. Randall Long


All rights reserved

# *Forward*

People have asked me why I am writing a book such as this...what is the purpose and what do you expect to accomplish? At first it gave me pause. Why *am* I writing this and does it really need to be written? At first I suppose I just wanted to get some things off my chest, perhaps vent my frustrations and make myself feel a little bit better. We all know that at times it is good to express our feelings.

After watching the news, reading the newspaper or perusing the internet I felt compelled to get some things down on paper, to verbalize the feelings, concerns and fears that were running through my mind.

Finally, after being asked many times and having to consciously rationalize it I came up with what I hope is the ultimate outcome and purpose of this book.

I do not want conflict or controversy; rather I want constructive discussion, dialogue and debate. I really desire that people simply take the time to ponder, question and ask themselves and others questions about where are as a country and why we are in this place? But the larger and more pertinent question is what can we do about it?

We still live in the greatest country in the world, but America did not attain this distinction by accident. Our greatness was predicated on a lot of very special, intelligent, enlightened and dedicated men and women who desired something better. I happen to believe that we still have special, intelligent, enlightened and dedicated men and women today who care about this republic and are willing to make a difference, who are willing to demand accountability and to be held accountable.

# Acknowledgements

I was fortunate to receive an extraordinary amount of help, support and encouragement in the completion of this book. It is my first undertaking of anything close to this project and my heartfelt thanks goes out to all those who contributed.

My Thursday night Writers Group: without their support and encouragement I would have thrown in the towel long ago;

My two editors, Sue and Kate: they are the real brains behind the scene;

And finally, to all my friends and family who encouraged me to step out and do something I have never done before.

# Chapter 1 - Introduction
# I Am Afraid and
# Perhaps You Should Be

I am mad as hell. To top it off I am experiencing an increasingly high level of anxiety and uneasy fear for one of the few times in my life. It is a deep and pervasive kind of fear, alternating with anger and frustration, counter to my norm of optimism and trust. My belief is that we are in serious trouble. I can count on one hand the times in my life when I have been frightened, but never exactly like this. I am not so fearful for myself, but more for my children and grandchildren. It is not comforting to know that I am not alone in my apprehension and discomfort. There seems to be a great many ordinary people who share my concerns and that, in and of itself, validates my view that I am not alone. When in doubt turn to Webster:

*Free Pass*

*Fear* - alarm and agitation caused by the expectation or realization of danger. A state of dread or apprehension.

That is exactly what I am experiencing right now and I venture a guess that there are a lot of you having that same experience. I now look at most elections with the belief that people on both sides are fearful of what might transpire. Should we not be comfortable and optimistic that, regardless of the outcome, we will be in good hands? Should we not be able to be confident that the future is bright and that we have leaders who care about the common good and will focus their efforts on repairing the problems and strengthening our nation? I want a media I can trust, and who will be a watchdog. I want a media that is objective and unbiased, who brings true news that is not slanted or filtered, and is above all else, honest. I want the entertainment and professional sports industries to clean up their acts, to become socially responsible and to become accountable. I want our large corporations to balance profits with social responsibility and trust. I want our education system to again become world class and to set the standard. I want our legal and penal system to do what it is expected to do.

I see a vehicle careening wildly out of control at ever-increasing speeds directly toward a chasm, and no one seems able or willing to stop it or even slow it down. This is the same vehicle I have viewed as under cruise control and driven by highly competent, safe and dependable stewards. There is a great debate going on right now as to whether this country is still great or not. As for me, I think it is both a matter of degree and of specific area. We are certainly still a great country, as evidenced by all of the people who want to come here. But are we still the elite world force? Are we economically, militarily, and culturally the country we once were, and could still be? Are we on an upward trend, simply holding our own, or slowly but surely sliding down a slippery slope? Do we still hold the respect and trust we once enjoyed on the world stage? Does the world at large still look to us for leadership, or do they see a country in disarray: chaotic and divided? Do we still enjoy the same level of respect, trust and optimism that we have enjoyed in the past? Are we as prosperous and economically vital as we were? And lastly, are we the country others emulate and look up to as the land of opportunity? I am not one to subscribe to conspiracy theory or even engage in negative conjecture about things like politics, big business, the legal system, or the way things work in general. I am not an alarmist. I have trusted the system and for the most part the people who run it. I always had faith that they were intelligent, mostly honest, and above all, interested in our, the people's welfare. Lately, I have become increasingly concerned that my faith is unfounded, misplaced and that we as a nation, and our future, are in very serious trouble in almost all facets of our lives. I have deep and abiding concerns about everything from sports to politics, from business to the legal system,

*Free Pass*

and from the media to the entertainment industry. Accountability seems to be a term on the verge of extinction in our everyday society.

A Texas teenager steals cases of beer from a Wal-Mart store, proceeds to get drunk (reportedly three times the legal blood alcohol limit), then speeds 70 miles per hour with friends loaded in the bed of his pickup truck. He plows into a group of people, including a youth pastor who has stopped to help a stranded motorist. In all, four people died at the scene and several were injured. A young man riding in the back of the teen's truck was paralyzed. The teen then fled the scene before being captured by police.

It is noteworthy that his parents are wealthy and this was not his first offense - both significant points. It is a clear example of where accountability and consequences should be in evidence. Between an uncaring and probably incompetent judge, a creative defense attorney, and money and power, accountability did not even come into play. His defense was that he was a victim of "affluenza" ... the cultural by-product of wealthy, privileged parents who set no boundaries or guidelines. So, because his parents never expected any accountability, he basically got exempted from any consequences. The judge told him, "It's not your fault; you can do whatever you want. There will be no penalties or consequences."

This is our justice system at its best! Freeing an arrogant and spoiled teen brat from any responsibility, consequences or accountability is unacceptable. Ask the victims' families if accountability or justice was even considered. How can anyone read this and not be angry, scared and frustrated?

A personal story is relevant at the other end of the spectrum, but also a tale of accountability, or lack thereof.

While sitting in my car outside a grocery store, a pair of middle-aged women accompanied by a young boy approached the car parked beside mine. Since my car was facing in the opposite direction to theirs and my window was down, my view was unobstructed, as was my ability to hear very clearly what was about to happen.

The woman who was the driver opened her door and got into the driver's seat, while her companion did the same on the other side. The young boy, probably 11 or 12 years old, opened the rear door on the driver's side as if he was throwing open the gate at a rodeo and banged his door into the side of my car. It was not only visually very evident, but it also left nothing to the imagination in the way of sound. You know: the sound of metal banging against metal. Upon examination there was an indentation in the side of my new car the size of a silver dollar.

The woman, who was obviously the mother, ignored the whole thing, in spite of her window being down as well.

I then asked the inevitable question, "Are you not aware that your son just dented my car with his door?"

The kid's eyes grew as wide as saucers and the look on his face gave instant testimony that he knew exactly what he had done. I expected an immediate acknowledgement and apology, and perhaps an admonishment for the child and maybe even an apology from him. What I received was an indignant denial from the mother that her son had done anything inappropriate, and she insisted that I was wrong.

On the surface this seems a rather insignificant event, and certainly not in the same realm or magnitude as the previous story. Granted, it is not. It probably happens hundreds of times daily in cities and towns across the country, although typically without the offender being caught red-handed.

On a deeper level, I believe it is symptomatic of a more pervasive problem, one which is being played out on a much grander scale. This is where the two stories converge in an ugly truth. In that single moment, the mom sent a very clear message to her son, just as the parents and judge in the former story did, that it is perfectly all right to duck accountability. That they are the real victims and there are no consequences to one's actions if you simply ignore them. You can dodge them, deny them, or better yet hire an expensive attorney and use your resources to buy your way out of trouble.

As I pen this book and as I become even more aware of the seeming demise of accountability, I have grown increasingly fearful and concerned about what is transpiring in this historically great country of ours. Perhaps I have become more sensitive and more vigilant, but the examples seem to be coming in rapid-fire succession on a daily basis. It has come to be all too easy to spot people, politicians, companies and organizations who have adopted the dodging of accountability as a way of life and as a given in their conduct. Accountability has evolved into such a throw-away and irrelevant artifact that a lot of people just accept the ignoring of it as a way of life. In some circles it has become an art form.

You may be asking why I am so concerned about accountability and why I am so fearful about its demise. My belief is that it is a tangible and visible symptom of the health and welfare of our society and culture. If we continue on this path we are vulnerable in some very dangerous areas. Specifically, we must restore accountability in our local, state and federal governments, starting with our elected officials. We must restore accountability in our legal, penal and justice systems. We must restore accountability in the media, entertainment and professional sports. Yes, I said professional sports. And last, but not least, we need corporate accountability.

My intent is not to complain and vent, but rather to suggest some possible solutions. What I would really welcome and relish is sparking a dialogue. I would feel a very real sense of accomplishment if conservatives, liberals, independents and everyone else who cares about this country, its future and our children's future began to find common ground to fix this incredible mess we are in. We can and should start with the cesspool we call Washington, D.C. It is a quagmire of partisanship, corruption, inefficiency, ineffectiveness and insider dealings. These are harsh words, but I believe the evidence is overwhelming. It has become a *country club* of career politicians, lobbyists and others whose only investments are self-serving.

Admittedly my chapters will contain my own personal opinions, values and observations, but I will try to balance that with facts, statistics and examples.

I am continually frustrated that the media and politicians purport to speak for me, the everyday man (or woman as the case may be). I want to express my own opinion about issues that matter to me. I just do not have the same bully pulpit that the aforementioned media and politicians have. How often do you get to hear from the person on the street regarding the economy, national security, immigration, justice, or other critical issues? I am sick and tired of people assuming to speak for me.

How many of you reading this book have guaranteed lifetime jobs? Not many, I would assume. Yet we have people in key places who have just that: immunity from accountability because they cannot be fired or dismissed, other than for gross offenses.

Is there justification for a college professor to have tenure? Where did this come from and who thought it up? Do you think there is any chance whatsoever that a tenured professor at a state university feels any sense of true accountability? Do you think the Supreme

Court Justices or federal judges care one whit about accountability? How about federal employees in general? Do you think there are a lot of them who are really concerned about performance as it relates to their job security? I have a lot of love and respect for teachers and generally believe they are dramatically underappreciated and undercompensated. I also recognize the fact that it is extraordinarily difficult to get rid of the low and marginal performers. The fundamental question is, should anyone be bulletproof and given full immunity from accountability or anything akin to it?

Before you read on, and in the true spirit of disclosure and accountability, I should disclose a bit of my background, philosophy and frame of reference.

I grew up in a bit of an anomaly. My mom and dad were very blue collar conservatives, but were Democrats. I managed to make it through six years of college without my spiritual or political views having ever been assaulted questioned or even tested.

I served in the military as a survival instructor during the Vietnam war. I spent most of my career in the corporate world, and was fortunate to be in positions as an objective observer from the very top to the very bottom. I was even asked to do things that were unethical and probably even borderline illegal, although I declined. I have worked in the energy sector, the high tech sector, the retail sector and even the public school sector. In each of these I gained some very interesting and valuable insights.

I have always tried to analyze situations objectively and to look at things from every point of view, but as I write this book I am continually questioning my objectivity. In a great many situations the reality seems to jump out at me so powerfully that I struggle to rationalize what I see.

Some personal criteria and biases:

I am a strong supporter of and defender of the Constitution.

I am a fan of transparency.

I expect good character, integrity and honesty.

I love debate and respect contrary opinions.

I assume the best in other people until they prove otherwise.

I respect people the most who accept accountability and responsibility.

I do not respect those who say things, but do not execute on them.

My greatest hope is that the following chapters challenge you to look at things objectively, with an open and challenging mind, and to discuss and debate the issues. To be critical thinkers and listen carefully to issues.

We have two choices: we can concede and do nothing and hope things take care of themselves, or we can get engaged, be proactive and demand positive changes. Above all else, we need to eliminate or at least minimize the *Free Passes*.

If we fail to wake up, recognize what is going on and begin to take action, I am concerned that my fears are going to culminate in a scenario that is ultimately irreversible, and one which will make the Republic only a chapter in our history books.

I will warn you, the deck is stacked against us in trying to clean this mess up. It is going to take the will of the people and the grit and determination of the full force of the American electorate to effect positive change and restore accountability. We cannot count on the current incumbent politicians, the political party machines, or the media to help. They are all invested in the way things are and in the way things are headed.

We have a two-party system, which has served us well from the beginning, but it has evolved into a two-headed monster. It is virtually impossible to identify anyone who we can trust to restore order, decency, honesty, character and leadership. No one wants to be held accountable.

# Chapter 2 - Politicial System The Best That Money Can Buy

Ask yourself two questions:

1. Why did America become the nation that it is, or at least was?

2. Would the founding fathers of this country be happy with the current state of affairs?

Pondering these and other questions like them on a recurring basis I am frustrated, angry, disillusioned, and feeling a bit helpless. I am a committed voter and even contact my elected officials on occasion, but my faith and confidence that I can make a difference has gone out the window, along with my faith and trust in them. My feeling is that there are a tremendous number of people who feel exactly like me.

I want to wake up each day confident in the fact that we have people at the helm who genuinely care about not just me, but the common good. I want to be confident that regardless of who is in power, we have leaders who will put aside personal or party agendas, who can debate and compromise, who can problem-solve and consider all alternatives, and who can come up with answers and solutions that are not driven by any ideology or personal bias, or worse yet, any special interest group, but rather by what is in the best interests of the country. Is this out of the realm of being a reasonable expectation?

Did the founding fathers envision a republic of partisan politicians continually bickering, fighting, and promoting selfish agendas? Or, did they envision a group of unselfish, intelligent, and enlightened individuals with an agenda serving the common good?

The founders set up a system of checks and balances to help ensure equity, fairness, and safeguards--not a system to be violated by any group intent on having its own way. The wisdom of the founders was to create equable and quality decisions to benefit the majority of Americans. This basic but well thought out system has been abused, violated, and distorted. Why and how has this been allowed to happen?

First ask yourself this question: do you think it was even in the realm of thinking of the founding fathers that we would have career politicians? Do you think they envisioned one man or one woman sitting in Congress for twenty, thirty, or even forty years? Is this healthy? If not, why not?

Next, did the founders envision lobbyists representing special interest groups exerting influence over lawmakers by spending time, money, and resources that you and I cannot afford? Additionally, we do not have the same access to elected officials that lobbyists have. Do you think lobbyists care about the best interests of the majority, or some narrow, well-funded group?

Let me stop here and insert a real life example. On at least two occasions I have felt compelled to voice an opinion and ask questions of one of my senators. She is not a member of the party that I typically vote for, but I have always voted for her because I believed in what she seemed to represent. I am not so naïve as to expect a personal response, but I did expect at least to receive a response remotely close to the subject I had addressed. Instead, I received a response so off the subject that it was insulting and disrespectful. I was totally disillusioned and angry.

Am I being represented? The bottom line, I believe that no true accountability exists. If it did, we would not have career politicians from both parties in Washington for decades. They get comfortable, arrogant, and self-serving. The perks become an aphrodisiac. They become ingrained with their own agenda and sense of power. They become indebted to the powers that contribute to their election and to the special interest lobbyists who stroke their egos and pad their lifestyles.

Ponder this question: if we had the same actors in Washington at the founding that we have now, could they replicate the same republic that we now enjoy? Could they collaborate, compromise, and problem solve to form a "more perfect union"? Could they come together to agree to "establish justice, to insure domestic tranquility, to provide for the common defense, and to promote the general welfare"?

My business background taught me several things in life which appear to be diametrically opposed to the way things are done in government at both the state and national level. Of course, in business there has always been a sense of accountability. There always a "pay for performance" system and consequences for not getting the job done. I was taught such things as collaboration, compromise, and complex and creative problem solving. The concept called "win-win negotiations" has been lost by the politicians and bureaucrats and replaced by a zero-sum game. I get extraordinarily frustrated when I see issues tackled unilaterally, following a political platform, agenda, or philosophy.

A recent piece of legislation is an example. There is absolutely no doubt in my mind that there was an urgent and dire need for healthcare reform. But who among us truly and honestly believes we can trust the federal government to single-handedly reform and administer a national healthcare program? In particular, how could this be accomplished by one political party? There is a ridiculous amount of bureaucracy, complexity, and cost associated with the final product. Ask your doctor what he or she thinks. It is a well-known fact that basically none of the members of congress who voted for the bill actually read the bill. How can this fact even be rationalized? Do we not supposedly elect intelligent, responsible and ethical individuals whose primary job it is to not only write sound legislation but to also read legislation written by others, especially when they are supposed to vote on it? How else can one determine the validity and soundness of said legislation?

Would it not have been better to get all of the representative players together, including doctors and hospitals, insurance companies, drug companies, and, yes, even the trial lawyers, to at least make an effort to hammer out some reforms that would work? If you think the federal government is qualified to administer a universal healthcare program, just take a look at the Veterans' Administration, the United States Postal Service, the Social Security Administration, and Medicare.

Have you asked yourself lately why you voted for a particular candidate? Was it because you remember him or her from an ad you saw or heard or perhaps a yard sign? Was it because of their party affiliation or platform? I have been asking myself that same question for the last few years and it has generated more questions than answers. To whom are they obligated? Are they career politicians? What are their real qualifications? Why are they running for office and what is their real agenda? Are they willing to negotiate in good faith and compromise when appropriate, except when it comes to ethics and integrity?

Are they problem solvers and collaborators? Finally, are they more interested in the common good or an agenda set by themselves or their political party? My own belief is that the president and members of congress should first and foremost conform to the precepts of being good leaders. For a great deal of my corporate career I taught development classes on leadership and have had ample opportunity to research, study and ponder what makes a great leader. You undoubtedly have your own ideas about what a great leader looks like and how he or she behaves. Allow me to share some characteristics I have gleaned over the years. It is not a perfect list and some of the ideas are up for debate and interpretation.

• First, a good leader must be a good follower. This concept entails a sense of humility and understanding the needs of those being led. By default, it means being able to change one's mind in the face of new and changing circumstances and being willing to admit when you are wrong.

• A great leader is self-confident without being arrogant, and truly humble when the circumstances warrant. Somehow our elected officials have come to believe that this is a sign of weakness and of being disloyal to the party.

• Great leaders are decisive and inspire confidence in their decisions.

• They build teamwork through consensus and collaboration.

• They always have a plan, are able to communicate that plan, and then inspire others to help execute the plan.

*Free Pass*

• They are creative problem solvers and encourage others to be problem solvers by requiring that others bring potential solutions.

• They are great communicators, not great orators with hollow messages that are ineffective.

• Leaders focus on results and then hold accountable those responsible, while being held accountable themselves.

• Leaders know how to delegate, gather relevant information and facts, and then make informed decisions that best serve the needs of the organization or constituency.

• Leaders typically do not have spines that are al dente. They do not abuse their power but are prone to action and getting things done.

• They are advocates for those being led.

• Above all else they are held to the highest ethical standards in their conduct and practices.

It does not take a great leap to transfer these characteristics to our elected officials, both the president and members of congress. Assuming that some if not most individuals we elect possess at least some of these characteristics when elected, why does the car run off the road when they get to Washington? Why does collaboration, creative problem solving, compromise and constructive communication get swept to the side?

It is my belief that several things happen, not necessarily in any order. We have allowed and perhaps even encouraged a polarization of opinion, philosophy and thought that demands strict adherence.

We have condoned and empowered career politicians who have lost sight of what their roles, responsibilities and mandates really are. In short, we have removed accountability and the thought of accountability. They have become so ensconced in the trappings associated with the job that they have abandoned the real mission, and instead focus on re-election. I do not use the word trappings lightly.

Here is a partial list of the perks enjoyed by congressional members:

You can start with the power to shape policy and public discourse, pretty heady stuff and something that a person could get caught up in and perhaps even lead to an indebtedness. The salaries are high by middle class standards, but not unreasonable based on what is expected, although not always delivered.

Here is a breakdown of the base compensation of our top elected officials:

| | |
|---|---|
| President | $200,000 |
| Vice President and | |
| President Pro Tempore | $193,400 |
| Speaker of the House | $223,500 |
| Majority and Minority Leaders | $193,400 |
| All other Representatives | $174,000 |
| Office expense | |
| allowances range | $121,049 to $453,828 |
| Administrative and clerical | |
| assistance range | $2,361,820 to $3,753,614 |

I am not saying these are out of line, but how does anyone know? I am simply saying that it is a definite inducement to hold onto the job. Each senator is also authorized a minimum of $40,000 for furniture and furnishings in his or her home state office, which can increase based on the size of the office. By the way, they get free office space in a federal building in their home state. I am not saying it is bad in and of itself, but it begins to add up as an inducement for a lifetime gig. Of course they get hefty pension benefits after only five years, and a unique medical plan not available to the rest of us and not a part of what they have created and imposed on us.

House Speaker Boehner has really made out like a bandit after a mere 23 years. In addition to his $223,000 salary he will receive, by law (and guess who passed the law) an additional benefit. After he finally leaves office he will receive up to one million dollars per year for up to five years. He claims this is not frivolous spending, but serves to facilitate the administration, settlement and conclusion of matters pertaining to or arising out of his tenure as Speaker of the House.

This same provision in the law has enriched the former Speaker Denny Hasert, to the tune of $997,000 over the course of three years, at the last accounting. At this juncture can you begin to see a pattern of no accountability and perhaps why we cannot as a nation balance the budget? We have a large group of privileged people gorging themselves at the trough of taxpayer donations; a trough they are very reluctant to give up. After all, there is no real accountability since they themselves are the creators and maintainers of that trough.

There is even more. They get free postage to deluge us with material telling about all that they have accomplished, which in reality is campaigning for the next election.

Lawmakers also get special amenities with the airlines and airports, all of which can be directly affected by legislation and rules. Airlines permit legislators to make multiple reservations but use only one, with no extra cost. They also get free reserved parking at the two DC airports. And to top it off they have a free on-site gym, and because they work so hard and get so much accomplished they get up to 239 days off.

I am not arguing that any of this is excessive, although it could be. I am merely saying that when they are elected they come face to face with the golden goose. If you add in the lobbyist benefits and perks, it adds up to a strong desire for a lifetime job. Term limits would certainly build in some level of accountability and a more focused effort on performance and results -- results for the general welfare of the country -- which would definitely add accountability.

I stated earlier that the people who become our president and members of congress must be good leaders. Let me add something, our national leaders must lead in the fight to preserve and defend our constitution.

*Free Pass*

Our leaders have become complacent, perhaps even complicit in a lot of areas, but probably none as dramatic and profound as money management, the use and abuse of our hard-earned tax dollars. We have probably all heard the occasional example of the boondoggle, but allow me to cite some really extreme examples of how out of control the spending and mismanagement has become:

• A startling $37 million was spent as an initial inquiry for the US to suppress increasing unrest in the Middle East by "having everyone pretend to convert to Islam for a year or two."

• $1.9 million was lost in taxes due to the ill-advised one-year extension of the "Too Tired to Work" credit.

• $4 billion (yes that's billions) in funding issues to those states who improperly achieve a double benefit on federal Medicaid payments.

• We spent $1.2 million to study whether eating radioactive tuna resulting from the Fukushima disaster will result in humans with mild superpowers.

• $171,000 was spent to teach monkeys to gamble in order to determine if monkeys, like humans, believe in the idea of a "hot hand."

• $473,000 of your dollars was spent to put 100 chimpanzees in a room with 100 typewriters for a year to determine whether, given sufficient time, they could recreate the complete works of Tucker Max.

• $387,000 was spent to decide the effects that robot-provided massage has on the physical recovery of rabbits after exercise.

• The military was given $1 billion in order to destroy $16 billion in unnecessary purchases of ammunition.

• The military was also awarded $21 million for the Army Corp of Engineers to rebuild buildings that continue to burn down because of shoddy construction.

• And by the way, the military spent $80 million to develop an actual Ironman suit.

• There was $371,000 earmarked to study if mothers loved their dogs as much as their own kids.

• You spent $307,000 to determine the impact schools of swimming Sea Monkeys have on ocean current.

• There was $4.2 billion lost to fraudulent tax refunds issued to identity thieves.

• $10 million was lost in tax revenue by allowing the super-rich to rent their homes for up to two weeks each year tax-free.

• There is $331,000 to study if the concept of "hunger" is real by testing if hungry spouses are more likely to stab a voodoo doll representing their significant other.

• $820,000 to determine the impact that public breastfeeding has on the rate of car accidents at crowded intersections.

• $100,000 for the Coast Guard to patrol some of the country's most exclusive real estate to stop uninvited guests from crashing private parties.

• $194,000 to determine if automatic text messages can encourage heavy drinkers to stop boozing. Of course it does not take a rocket scientist to see the inherent problem with this one, potentially sending a text to a heavy drinker while he is driving … duh.

• $2.6 million was spent training Chinese prostitutes to drink more responsibly on the job.

• More than $13 billion in Iraq aid has been classified as wasted or stolen, and another $7.8 billion cannot be accounted for.

• I will end the examples with this one: $120,000 was paid in performance bonuses to an Environmental Protection Agency employee who admitted to viewing porn for up to six hours a day on government computers.

Can anyone argue that there is massive abuse of the federal budget, the budget funded by our tax dollars? It is a recognized fact that tax dollars are mismanaged, wasted and misappropriated. It is a problem so widespread and prevalent that our elected officials have decided that it is easier to just look the other way and ignore it. They have chosen to ignore accountability.

As a matter of fact, politicians are contributors to the problem. Legislation is enacted that is full of pork and entails ridiculous spending on absurd things to appease special interest groups in their home state or lobbyists in Washington. This course of action ignores the common good in favor of a few. What if politicians were like NASCAR drivers, in that they had to adorn their jackets and cars with patches and decals depicting which lobbyists, big donors and special interest groups have made big donations to them?

There are literally thousands of examples of misspent dollars in the budget. There has to be a way to clean this mess up. We can no longer afford the luxury of throwing our hands up and saying it is just too big and too complex. In the corporate world when there was a need to cut costs and realign priorities we did something called zero-based budgeting. That meant that we built a budget from the ground up. We had to make tough decisions about how we would spend the dollars. We had to prioritize what was really necessary and what we could live without. We were held accountable for justifying what we included in our budget.

The results were usually quite astonishing. We became creative in ways to get things done with less, and the savings were incredible. The federal budget, and in fact the state budgets, are just the opposite. Since there is no real accountability, there is apparently a rolling budget. Last year's dollars are assumed valid and new dollars are just added to accommodate the bureaucracy.

Speaking of the bureaucracy, do you have any idea how difficult it is to discipline, much less terminate, a federal or state worker for poor performance? Our elected officials have created a behemoth of a Frankenstein when it comes to the workforce. You tell me, what is the level of efficiency and customer service you get when contacting one of these elite agencies? Have you ever had the expressed urge to shout out, "I am a taxpayer and I pay your salary!" Has a beast been created that can never be controlled and reined in to accountability?

Friends, we are in a very dangerous time in our history. We have enemies at our gates who want to cause great harm to us and our loved ones. We have monumental issues both internal and external that can result in grave consequences for not only us, but our descendants. We can no longer afford career politicians who are comfortable, who bicker and fight, and who feel no sense of accountability. We can no longer tolerate elected officials who refuse to answer a simple yes or no question with a simple yes or no answer just because it would be a sign of transparency and accountability. We can no longer justify sending people to Washington or the state capital without strong leadership qualities. We need people who can unify, collaborate, inspire and rally us; people who command respect not only from us but from the world at large.

Speaking of the world, we need a strong coalition of support and unity from our trusted allies, a coalition which has not been seen since World War II. We must have leaders who can inspire confidence and trust in America, leaders who can rally a level of common purpose that is insurmountable by the bad guys in the world today. We must get in front of the dangerous issues, confront them and deal with them from a position of strength.

Like it or not, America has always led the fight for things like freedom, justice, and peace. We need leaders who can stand the test of accountability domestically as well as internationally. We need leaders who take a stand, problem solve, and then take appropriate action, calculating the risk as well as the consequences of not taking action. We need leaders who are masters at building consensus and collaboration, especially with our allies.

I believe our allies are just waiting for America to stop procrastinating, bickering, and fighting amongst ourselves and step up as world leaders again. They want America to be accountable on the world stage, but more so, to hold others accountable, a role cast upon us by history.

I do not have a PhD in world affairs, political science or any other related discipline, but I do have some thoughts when it comes to the security, stability and general welfare of this country, as well as the other countries we count as allies. I am not a big fan of the UN (United Nations). Is it really an organization of nations who are united and who are accountable to no one? There are so many questionable members in the UN that it is a joke. The UN is the equivalent of forming a neighborhood watch group and asking the local burglar, gang member and assorted thugs to join as members and to vote on security measures. We waste tremendous amounts of money on an organization that is ineffective, inefficient and has, in general, outlived its usefulness. Where are they on the issue of ISIS?

We live in a very dangerous world. It is also a complex and different world than the one most of us grew up in. It is increasingly difficult to separate the good guys from the bad, but unfortunately our very future depends on it. We need a coalition or organization of countries who pledge a common purpose or mission, to fight terrorism, oppression and social injustice.

A pledge must be made to do this through economic sanctions, collaboration, and if absolutely necessary, force. Above all, it must have accountability through results. We, the United States of America, need to take the lead role. Like it or not, it is a role cast upon us because of who we are, or at least who we have been. We can speculate, we can debate or even argue, but this country is something special. It is not a boast and it is not arrogant, it is just a plain fact.

Are you beginning to see why we need leaders who are actual leaders, not politicians who care more about money, power and their own security? We must have people who think and process problems creatively and in new ways. We cannot afford the same old familiar faces and platforms, who are content with business as usual.

The next time we approach elections please think ACCOUNTABILITY. Have they shown accountability as a trait? Are they willing to be held accountable for results? Do they have the right kind of experience, skills, leadership and above all else character to be the CEO of the greatest country in the world?

Here is my personal checklist going into the next election:

• Is the candidate a committed protector and upholder of the Constitution of the United States of America?

• Does the candidate have unimpeachable character? If and when they do err, as almost everyone does, do they step up, admit it and apologize?

• Will they pledge to be totally transparent in everything they do? If you have nothing to hide, transparence should be a given.

• Will they respond to direct questions with direct answers, not political speak?

• Will they work for the common good, not special interests, political parties, some personal ideology or lobbyists?

• Will they work to begin to attack government waste, frivolous spending and to reduce costs?

• Will they work on the tax code, to simplify it and make it equitable-everyone pays their fair share, including the wealthy?

• Are they committed to term limits and will they work diligently toward that goal?

• Will they work with business leaders and entrepreneurs to figure out a strategy to get this economy running the way it is supposed to run? To create jobs, opportunities and economic prosperity? To give everyone who wants to work the opportunity to work and to succeed?

*Free Pass*
- Will they work to figure out a solution to the illegal immigration problem? This country is a country of immigrants because we developed a logical, orderly and above all else, legal process. What exactly is there about the term "Illegal" that the people in Washington do not understand?
- Will they work on legislation to limit access by lobbyists and special interest groups and to make public and transparent all interactions and dealings with those individuals and groups?
- Will they work towards campaign spending limits? Campaigns should be won on factors other than out-spending the opponent.
- Will they work on legislation prohibiting the use of Air Force One and other government resources for political fund raising?
- Will they work on a legal and fair process of performance management, performance appraisal and discipline for federal and state employees, as the case may be? We need "Pay for Perfomance."
- Are they willing to collaborate, compromise appropriately and problem solve?
- Will they speak the truth ... regardless of the consequences?
- ARE THEY WILLING TO BE ACCOUNTABLE?

In short we need to scrutinize, analyze and examine all political candidates in ways we perhaps have never done before. We can no longer afford to be passive spectators; we have to get in the game. The futures of our children and grandchildren are literally on the line. We have to listen intently to candidates' messages and listen with all of our intuitive abilities.

Are they giving us political speak or a genuine, honest and relevant message, better yet answers? Do they have solutions, ideas and plans or is most of their rhetoric centered on slamming the opposing side? We need to get actively involved by looking for every opportunity to ask the tough and relevant questions. Write letters and emails, attend meetings, and talk to local political party leaders, write letters to the editors, and telephone in.

Best of all, if given the chance, ask the candidate face-to-face . I can remember a few years ago the Daughters of the American Revolution sponsored a "meet the candidate" event in our local park, where we could meet and speak with candidates for state office. I asked one particular candidate a very pointed question which was of great importance to me. He refused to answer the question. Of course this spoke volumes to me and not only about the specific issue at hand.

I for one am sick and tired of the mudslinging, the snide jokes, the innuendo and general bashing of the opposition. It shows a lack of class, a lack of professionalism and I believe a lack of confidence in their own abilities. I believe this is because they do not have definitive solutions so they try to deflect attention to the deficiencies of others.

In short, we need to give greater attention to who is running the country than who is running the local sports team, who is starring in the latest movie or who is posting on Facebook.

Both parties are guilty of focusing on numbers (the majority) rather than quality. We have lost accountability in the political equation and we must restore it and turn the corner before it is too late.

# Chapter 3 - The Media Can You Trust The Fourth Estate?

A good friend of mine who worked in public relations once told me, "Do not pick fights with anyone who buys ink by the railroad tanker car." I guess I am about to test the wisdom of those words, although I am not picking a fight, just making some points.

Everyone is biased and most have an opinion. Buying a car one makes a choice. They are biased toward a make, model, and color. Buying a home one makes decisions based on the style of home, the amenities, and the neighborhood. We all form opinions and biases based on a lot of factors. So I believe it is safe to assume that we all make choices and decisions based on our personal biases.

Do you really want to pick up a newspaper article (you remember newspapers, don't you?), read something on the internet, or tune in to a newscast and expect it to be totally biased, subjective and contain only personal opinion? Who is the media accountable to? Do they have a free pass? If we cannot trust or depend on the media where do we turn for factual, informative and trustworthy news and information, a great deal of which impacts our lives and livelihoods?

I remember people like Walter Cronkite, Mike Wallace and others who I trusted to report the truth based on the facts available. I believed there were reporters who investigated all issues, who probed for the truth and could be depended upon to ferret out the bad actors or actresses, regardless of who or what light was shined upon them. I don't remember comments about the "liberal press" or the "conservative press." It was just the press or just the news media.

Why do I have to choose between what is perceived to be the liberal channel or the conservative channel? Using the old tag line from the TV show Dragnet, "I want the facts, just the facts." I would like to tune in to basically any news channel, network or cable, and get the unvarnished truth on all stories and issues of relevance. I do not want to sort through whether the story is biased, opinionated or slanted. I do not want a story or issue completely omitted because it might shine a bad light on a particular party or elected official. What happened to the term journalistic integrity? I want the facts to speak for themselves, not filtered by opinion or bias. I simply want to make informed choices.

Character and integrity should be the standard. It recently came to light that a prominent journalist contributed a huge sum of money to a controversial foundation, a foundation that is under the microscope for some questionable donations in general. This journalist just happens to be a former advisor and staff member for the high profile political family whose foundation bears their name.

How could anyone even fantasize that this individual could report on this family in an objective, factual and unbiased manner? It is an insult to most intelligent people. Recently we had a very high profile and trusted news anchor embellish his experiences while on reporting assignments. It was a breach of trust and character severe enough to warrant his suspension. Prior to that a noted "newsman," one with a British accent, decided that it was so important to support his slanted opinion on a hot political issue that he should create a false statistic right on the spot. Not journalistic integrity at its best.

We have probably never seen political media bias to the extent that we saw during Barack Obama's campaign and election, and the love affair has not abated. Even the government's snooping of the Associated Press did not seem to change the slant. Do we really want the media facilitating the election of individuals? It is not unusual for a newspaper in the past to endorse a particular candidate, but it was typically done on the editorial page and with full disclosure. The current clandestine approach to giving a candidate preferential treatment is disgusting and unacceptable. The Washington Post's ombudsman admitted that the Post's coverage was biased strongly in favor of Obama and against McCain.

Lest you think this is just my opinion, the Gallup Poll has some interesting statistics on yours and my opinion of the media. Prior to Watergate in 1973, trust in the media had peaked at a point just above 70%. Since Watergate, trust in the media has steadily declined to an all-time low of 40%. Americans have lost confidence in the media to report the news fully, accurately, and fairly. To say it another way, a recent poll states that 60% of Americans distrust the media. Without having conducted a poll, I can only speculate as to why this decline has occurred. Watergate required a genuine interest in getting to the bottom of something and then employing some real investigative techniques and resources. Since then I believe the populace has gradually begun to realize that those same journalist qualities are no longer in play.

The very first amendment to the Constitution states, "Congress shall make no law respecting an establishment of religion, or prohibiting the free exercise thereof; or abridging the freedom of speech, or of the press; or the right of the people peaceably to assemble, and to petition the Government for redress of grievances."

Freedom of the press is a powerful right but it also implies a powerful obligation. It gives them great freedom of latitude, but I do not believe that it grants a free pass.

When the Constitution and its subsequent amendments were drafted, the framers had experience with a monarchy that quashed any such ideas of free speech and freedom of the press. If you look at dictators and most monarchies down through history it becomes evident that controlling the media is a primary concern. If you control the media and the message, you can control the people, or at the least, influence them.

I went to Wikipedia for the meaning and history of the term The Fourth Estate. "The Fourth Estate is a societal or political force or institution whose influence is not consistently or officially recognized. Fourth Estate most commonly refers to the news media, especially print journalism or the press. Thomas Carlyle attributed the origin of the term to Edmund Burke, who used it in a parliamentary debate in 1787 on the opening up of press reporting of the House of Commons of Great Britain. The term makes reference to the three Estates of the Realm.

"In current use the term is applied to the press, with the earliest use described by Thomas Carlyle in his book On Heroes and Hero Worship. Burke said there were three Estates in Parliament; but in the Reporter's Gallery yonder, there sat a Fourth Estate more important far than they all."

In some circles the Fourth Estate has evolved into the Fourth Branch, meaning that in essence there is a fourth branch of the government: the Legislative, the Judicial, the Executive, and the press or media. I will let you ponder this for yourself, but it gives me great concern that it is even being bantered about. I think historian John Buesher summed it up quite nicely. He stated, "Calling the media the fourth branch of government is a rhetorical device, not a serious statement of fact. The point is to emphasize that the press is not a mere passive reporter of the facts, but a powerful actor in the political realm. Calling it the fourth branch not only emphasizes the amount of power it wields, but is often meant to suggest that the power is not under the control of the people in the same way that their elected representatives are. The implication is that it acts as a shadow government, unaccountable to the people, but is instead beholden to special interests of one sort or another, or that the presses supposed separation from the government is largely an illusion. The corollary is that the press sometimes menaces rather than protects, or controls rather than serves, the public."

We all want to preserve that very precious first amendment right of free speech and freedom of the press. I believe that is a given. But what are the realistic expectations that can be placed on the media as a whole? Do they have free reign to distort, embellish, influence or be totally biased? If that is the case then they should join the tabloids at the grocery checkout counters. My belief is that we as a people are conflicted in our thinking. On one hand, if asked, we will very clearly and emphatically state that we do not trust the media, yet we still let them influence us.

Perhaps the better question might be what is the alternative?

The media's general lack of accountability is a huge concern to me on several fronts. First and foremost, I expect the media to be the accountability police. They are the ones who I have always counted on to hold others accountable: the politicians, the corporations, the judges and law enforcement - in other words, all those who are supposed to protect the public trust. The media is who I have counted on to dig in and ferret out what is going on behind the scenes, both the good and the bad.

Some very crucial elections are coming up in 2016 and I would sincerely like to have a media I can count on to help me sort through some extremely difficult decisions and issues. We are intelligent enough to make choices if we have good, accurate and unbiased information. We need information about experience, accomplishments, qualifications, philosophies, plans and strategies, and above all else, character and integrity. Commentary on transparency would be an added plus.

I am curious about the polls. We get pelted with all kinds of polls on every subject imaginable, including the one I quoted in this chapter. I have a hunch that a lot of people are influenced by these polls. They look at a poll and say, "Wow, if that many people feel that way, I must be out of step." They literally change their opinion on a person or subject because they want to be in step and in the mainstream. In all my years of experience I have never been involved in a poll. I do not even have a friend or relative who has been polled. My suggestion is that we take polls with a grain of salt and use them as one data point, but that we form our own independent opinions and not let them form our thoughts.

Finally, my last media irritation is the on-air talking heads pontificating on subjects from A to Z that most of them have no practical experience in. Quite frequently I find myself wanting to crawl through the television screen and express the opinion of a typical everyday person.

They also never, or very seldom, ask the obvious question or questions. For example it drives me crazy to see some talking heads, self-ordained oracles commenting on military issues as if they are experts, but have never served one single day. If they are a pacifist and do not believe in national security interests, just say so. "I am a pacifist, or isolationist, and have never served this country, and quite frankly I do not even have an alternative plan for national security."

One of my biggest concerns with the media is their ascension to the roles of social and cultural police. They have assumed the job of telling us what is politically correct and socially acceptable. Who exactly anointed them with this role? They have some other partners in this pursuit, namely college professors and the entertainment industry, but they have the continual open mike and are not reluctant to use it. Again, they pick and choose to whom and to what they apply their biased and mostly unwanted opinions. They profess to speak for everyone no matter the subject. I don't recall deciding who is going to speak for me when determining what is correct and acceptable and what is not.

My personal opinion is that the media, under the guise of political correctness, is seeking to dumb down free speech, deflect from the real issues, steer away from focusing on reality and in general trying to steer our thinking in another direction.

The media moguls are very sly and cunning. They understand incredibly well their power and reach and are not hesitant to use it at every opportunity to sway public opinion, whether it is for a political office holder, candidate, party, or social issue. I am mature and savvy enough to sort through the muck and bias and make up my own mind, but I am genuinely concerned about my descendants. Once the media, the college professors and the entertainment industry pile on, it becomes a pretty dismal picture and a decidedly lopsided agenda.

I watch the news channels in disbelief, regardless of which one it is. In an attempt to be balanced and objective they will sprinkle in "contributors"- purported journalists with opposing views and perspectives. Regardless of the facts and current evidence they steadfastly support the politician, candidate, and or party to which they have sworn allegiance. Is this an example of a journalist with character and integrity? Is this a person whom I can respect and count on to hold others accountable?

*Free Pass*

I do not want purveyors of the news to be doormats and pawns. I want them to look at the facts, the facts they are supposed to have researched, and come to a logical and fact based conclusion and report it. I sincerely believe that if a candidate or incumbent of their persuasion was caught stealing a car they would rationalize it somehow. Please do not insult our intelligence.

As much as I hate to see the media become extensions of political parties, advocates for political agendas and philosophies, and self-proclaimed social cops, I am at a loss as to how to solve the problem. The media is controlled by very wealthy individuals who have decided that they will use their wealth and power to promote their own agenda. They have abandoned the idea of journalistic integrity in favor of journalistic bias and power: pretty scary stuff. How do you balance freedom of speech with accountability? These wealthy individuals obviously have a financial dog in the fight and want to use their media empire to protect and enhance their own financial self-interests. There is little or no interest in what they are supposed to be about.

We owe a debt of gratitude to the media and to the reporters who persevered in discovering the facts behind Watergate. I am not so confident we can expect the same level of searching for the truth in today's environment. This is an extremely unfortunate commentary on today's society. The fortunate ones who have the access, the resources and talents to ferret out the issues and get to the unvarnished truth have all but decided that the seeking of total transparency is not in their job description. Said another way they are not held accountable and have chosen not to hold certain others accountable. As a result we are left without a media we can truly rely on and trust in general.

As this chapter is being penned there is a series of Presidential Candidate debates being conducted by some of the major networks. The most recent one stirred up a firestorm of controversy with accusations of bias and a generally bad job of debate structure and management. I watched at least parts of the debates and I have some questions that were never asked. I say this because it is my belief that most everyday Americans share some of my concerns. These are some of the simple and direct questions I would like to see asked of the candidates from both parties:

• Do you believe that we are better off as a country with career politicians running the country?

• Do you believe in transparency? Why is there so much stonewalling, avoidance and dodging of giving documents, data and answers to questions, assuming there is no guilt?

• What would you do to attack government waste and the associated spending?

• What is your strategy for dealing with the huge budget deficit and getting it under control?

• Do you feel that the Constitution is still a valid document, and if not, why not?

*Free Pass*

• Do you think there should be controls and limitations imposed on lobbyists and special interest groups, both in terms of finances and access?

• The world is a dangerous place. What would you propose doing to help ensure the safety and security of Americans here and abroad?

• Are you in favor of simplifying the tax code and making it fairer? If not, why not?

• What are the top three things you would do to stimulate job growth?

• Do you believe that "Big Government" is in the best interest of all Americans? If yes, why do you that?

• Do you believe that "Illegal" in the term "Illegal Alien" bears any credence? What should be done, specifically? Is it fair to the people who have gone through the legal process to ignore it?

• What is your stand on campaign spending limits?

• Who are your top campaign contributors?

Finally I would be remiss without mentioning social media. On one hand I am glad that free enterprise has endowed some young technology savvy entrepreneurs with great wealth. On the other hand I am very sad and concerned with the price it has exacted. I suppose that along with free speech comes a certain potential liability. At least in most forms of the media, one can claim slander and libel. In the social media there seems to be no real recourse. Peoples' names and reputations can be ruined in the blink of an eye with no real accountability. Pretty much anything can be implied, stated or even made up on the internet, with no real accountability or consequences. Your life is now pretty much an open book.

Unfortunately, it is my opinion that we no longer have an objective and unbiased source for even the simplest things. We have lost an advocate for the everyday American. An advocate who was a seeker of the facts. An advocate who held others accountable and held themselves to the highest standards. When the media loses credibility by seeking its own agenda, we are all in trouble, regardless of political and social views. You do not have to take my word for it; just look at history.

# Chapter 4 - Corporations Free Enterprise Is Not a Free Pass

Free enterprise: one of the cornerstones that made this country great. Free enterprise has created the opportunity, wealth and quality of life that most of us enjoy. It is synonymous with democracy and all that we hold dear. It has spawned an entrepreneurial spirit that has been the genesis of companies large and small, too numerous to count. It has allowed us to enjoy the benefits of all the things we take for granted. When we drive our car, when we use our appliances and our many technology devices, when we visit the physician of our choice and visit the pharmacy to obtain our medication, we are enjoying the fruits of free enterprise.

I can remember the first time I visited Hong Kong, knowing it was going to revert to the Chinese in a few years. Hong Kong was a vibrant city, teeming with the rewards of free enterprise. Would the Chinese government be willing to give up the benefits of this Western system to prove the merits of Communism? I made one subsequent business trip prior to the transition, but have not been back since. Based on what I have seen, read, and heard from others it appears that even the Chinese Communists comprehend the financial bottom line of free enterprise, albeit in a somewhat modified state.

Knowing what we know about the virtues of free enterprise, how can we reconcile the news we get on almost a daily basis regarding corporate improprieties? These include fraud, deception, and lying, but perhaps the worst is the wanton disregard for employees. More often than not, those employees worked hard and with loyalty to enable the organization to be successful.

We walk a fine line between insisting on more government intervention via rules, regulations, and policies and letting free enterprise work its magic. We do not want to even come close to stifling the entrepreneurial spirit, creativity, innovation or free enterprise. What we do want is accountability. Unfortunately, there will always be bad people doing bad things at the expense of others. Regrettably, we sometimes find them in positions of power and authority. We could devote an entire book and several psychologists to a discussion of why seemingly intelligent and successful individuals suddenly lose their moral compass. It is not relevant here. We are more interested in why they are not held accountable, criminally and/or financially, when they cause you and me to lose our retirement, our life savings, our future and our trust in the system.

We are supposed to have multiple entities, paid for with tax dollars, to guard and protect us from these free enterprise predators. You can call these individuals CEOs, CFOs, VPs, or board members. When they lie, misrepresent the facts, give themselves outrageous bonuses, commit fraud and deceive, they are no more than common criminals. We have the SEC, the FTC, the IRS and numerous other government agencies supposedly keeping a watchful eye and demanding accountability. Over-layering these crack teams of accountability seekers is the Justice Department and supposedly Congress. Lest we forget, members of Congress get help being elected by corporations and their lobbyists. Members of Congress get huge donations from corporations and their lobbyists during their election campaigns. So who is holding these folks accountable, the ones who are supposed to be holding others accountable?

One of the ironies you will find in this book is that there are many players in scores of different arenas who are woven into this rather complex tapestry of non-accountability. There are the offenders themselves, of course. Then there are the Board of Directors, the audit firms and auditors, the so-called regulatory agencies, the Justice Department and Congress. So pause for a moment, put the book down and think back to Enron and

WorldCom. Can you name, much less think of, very many individuals who were held accountable, either criminally or financially?

Now think about the recent mortgage debacle, the one precipitated by sub-prime lending. It triggered the greatest financial collapse in this country since the Great Depression. It not only affected this country, but dramatically impacted the world economy. The consequences are still being felt. Name someone, anyone, who has gone to prison over this huge financial nightmare. Good, hardworking people have lost their homes, their savings, and in some cases their families. Tangentially, many have lost their jobs and careers. Explain to me please why those responsible are still walking around and able to theoretically do the same thing again.

I saw an interview on one of the major network news programs with the head of the Justice Department, asking him this very question. He replied that it was a very complex issue and to stay tuned. Ask those folks who lost their homes and their savings how long they should stay tuned. If this situation does not warrant swift and decisive action to hold people accountable, then what does? It has been over six years. I know the wheels of justice turn slowly, but at least they are supposed to turn. If you owe the IRS back taxes, see if it will take six years for them to seize your assets and perhaps even prosecute you.

Now any logical person would assume the banks had learned their lesson, cleaned up

*Free Pass*

their act and instituted quality business practices. A rational person would also assume that the banks would feel a sense of remorse and feel compelled to clean up their tarnished image. The large banks have done just the opposite. It almost seems that they are on a vendetta to further punish those impudent swine who caused them all of this bad exposure. We will work with you, but it may take two or three years to make a final decision. In the meantime we are going to put you through hell on earth, orchestrated by some knucklehead who finished last in his high school class and believes customer service is an antiquated concept. I feel rather confident they were rejected by the airlines' customer service recruiters.

The airlines – those bastions of customer service and customer relations. Have you ever seen an industry, as a whole, which is more committed to poor customer service, deception and withholding information? If you are able to solve the riddle of airline pricing then we can put you on the world peace project.

I can remember taking my first commercial airline flight in 1970. It was a memorable trip to Lackland Air Force Base for basic training. I was so reluctant, frightened and dazed that customer service was the last thing on my mind.

Subsequent to that maiden voyage I logged over one and a half million miles. I cannot think of a major domestic airline I have not flown, as well as numerous regional and foreign carriers. I was gold, elite and preferred

M. Randall Long

on several airlines. All of this just means that I suffered through hundreds of bad experiences, some horrible. It means that I know firsthand how truly bad the domestic airlines really are.

I can remember sitting at a gate waiting many times and fantasizing that some entrepreneurial soul could start an airline with a true and honest focus on customer service. That this revolutionary airline would be honest about delays, both the cause and the length. They would not tantalize you by delaying in fifteen minute increments. They would not cram you in to seats made for people 4 foot tall and weighing 90 pounds. That they would not destroy a brand new piece of luggage and then tell you it is normal wear and tear.Then I awaken out of my fantasy by an announcement of my third gate change. (I have actually had as many as five)

Once I do board the airplane I walk toe to heal down an isle not much wider than a slug trail. I am then crammed into a seat that would be a tight fit for a Barbie Doll. To add insult to injury they are charging me a fee for my luggage, which by default is forcing my fellow travelers to try and fit more and bigger pieces of luggage into the overhead.

It will remain one of life's great mysteries why the airlines are apparently so committed to ignoring really quality customer service. Why, when fuel prices escalate, airline surcharges are quick to follow, but when fuel prices rapidly and precipitously decline, fares do not. Why airlines continue to cut service and amenities and figure out devious ways to gouge customers with fees and charges, all the while raising fares. Of course they know you can get so fed up you change carriers, but guess what, the other carrier is just as bad or worse. It is inconceivable to me that all of the airline executives are cut from the same cloth and apparently just do not care about the customer, except for their money, and their reputation. The so-called surveys of the best airlines are a laughing matter, tantamount to asking someone if they would rather have a heart attack or a stroke. I love the surveys reflecting on-time records...aren't they supposed to be scheduled airlines?

The airlines are horrible, but there is one industry that may have them beat. If someone says horrible customer service and customer relations, how long does it take for your mind to go to the cable companies? I can remember when cable television came into being. It was touted as the next great generation of home television entertainment, and the best part was NO COMMERCIALS.

I was watching a show recently, in reality it was a commercial interspersed with an occasional few minutes of programming. I stopped and counted 17commercials during at least one commercial break. Now let me get this straight. I pay over one hundred dollars a month for television and I still have to endure endless commercials. I am in fact paying to watch and be inundated with commercials. Many of the cable stations have even resorted to inserting these little popup crawlers across the bottom of the screen promoting their other programs. I find this annoying and distracting from the program, the one I am paying to watch. Between the monthly cable bill and all the money from commercials, where is all of this money going? It is not going to providing quality service.

Just recently I had a cable outage and spent an hour and fifteen minutes on the phone trying to get answers and solutions. When I finally did get a person, guess what? I could not understand them and they were of virtually no use in solving the problem. The airline executives would have been proud. A week later I had a problem with my internet service, which happens to be the same cable provider [fill in your local provider here]. You guessed it: 45 minutes on the phone trying to talk to three different people, none of whom had a real grasp of the English language. By the way, do they not justify sending customer service offshore to save money? Why have I not seen a commensurate saving on my bill?

A friend and business associate related another story, this one about a phone company which also provides DSL internet service. It is only fair to be balanced. The crew had come to my friend's neighborhood to work on an issue and ended up cutting their line. Of course it was on Christmas Eve morning. They refused to do anything until New Year's Eve, even though it was their fault. They even denied that it was their fault and also denied that they had been working in the neighborhood. Of course my friend had counted five trucks that day. They then

*Free Pass*

proceeded to tell them they would have to charge $80 to fix the problem, when they could get it on the schedule. When the crew did finally get around to it, they did some testing and said, "Yup, we sure did cut your line." They not only could not make or receive calls over the holidays, but her husband was unable to work from home.

I would suppose that the single biggest gut punch from the cable companies is their clever packaging of channels. I have not taken the time to count, but I have at least 100 plus channels, not counting music. Of these I might watch 25 at most, and that is being generous. There is no way I can just pick the 25 or so channels that I really want. They are all mixed and matched with other worthless channels that I am forced to bundle in. Some of the extraneous channels are even in languages I do not speak. You and I are forced to pay for something that is of no interest or use to us.

The cable companies are licensed by our local government entity and I would guess somehow regulated by the Federal Communications Commission, but who really holds them accountable? They are in essence a monopoly. Typically they control not only the cable television, but also the high speed internet connectivity. You can change to satellite television, if you are willing to be gouged for internet because you are not bundling services. In other words, you are willing to be punished, and still have the same TV program bundles.

There are also companies that have had such huge success they have become arrogant and totally out of touch with the customers who have contributed to their success. I am sure you have your own list, but I will give some of my own personal examples.

I was such a regular for so many years with a well-known national coffee chain that I felt like Norm on Cheers. The entire staff knew me by my first name and the manager gave me a Gold Card when they first came out. In the last year and a half several things became evident to me. The first being that the CEO has a particular political bent, which is fine, but it became evident he was intent on using his stores as social and political venues. I go there to get a quality cup of coffee, not be indoctrinated in his agenda.

Secondly I noticed a couple of things in the store that needed attention. Not to dwell on minutia but they refused to install a trash receptacle, in addition to the one in the condiment bar. On multiple occasions the trash was overflowing to the point that it was spread out on the counter and created what anyone would consider a sanitation issue. I emailed customer service and received a reply that was so off message it was insulting. I realized then that the company that I had been so loyal to was arrogant and could not care less what one customer brought to them. I used my personal coffee habit as accountability and have not been in one of their stores in almost two years. The side benefit is that I did not even realize how much

I was spending on over-priced coffee each month, and I have found a better and more cost-effective alternative. I am not suggesting that anyone follow suit, just that we can, as individuals hold companies accountable.

When one thinks of arrogance and thinks high tech one does not need to think further than Microsoft and Apple. I absolutely love it when I am shutting down my computer for the evening to go to bed, or rushing out the door to a meeting and Microsoft arbitrarily decides it is the right time to install 40 of 40 updates and the message comes up, "Do Not Shut Down or Unplug Your Computer." On the flipside, have you ever tried to get any simple answers to simple questions regarding your overpriced software? You can, but it will cost you, and good luck reaching anyone.

Apple is pretty much the same story, except they hold my cell phone hostage. My cell service provider is constantly telling me, "We cannot help you with that problem; you must go the Apple Store."

I am not totally sure one way or the other about GMO products, but until there is sufficient history to prove there are no adverse effects I am not willing to gamble my vital organs that it is okay. I grew up in Texas, the home of a major corn chip maker, and ate their chips most of my life. When the GMO question came up, I contacted them on their consumer 800 number. I was told by the woman on the help line that she could neither confirm nor deny the use of GMO corn. I asked, "Do you mean you cannot or will not"? She replied, "I will neither confirm nor deny the use of GMO corn." This sounded more like a Congressional hearing than a customer service discussion.

Needless to say, I stopped buying the chips and found a comparable, if not better chip at Trader Joe's. The best part is they are cheaper and clearly state on the package that they are NON-GMO. The chip company is not going to feel my loss of business, but I feel good that in some small way I am holding them accountable. By the way, I stopped buying any kind of chip from them.

About a year ago we went to a well-known national chain buffet restaurant. The experience was worse than horrible. They had numerous trays that were totally empty and others that had unappetizing remnants. When we questioned the staff, we got the same blank stare and a promise to fix the problem, which did not happen. When we got home, I emailed the company. The response was astonishing, in that there was no response at all. They are simply so arrogant and disinterested that any type of response is not even in their realm of thinking. You guessed it; I will never return. Accountability is not important to them, but it is to me. I have choices where I spend my money.

We hear a great deal about corporate greed, corruption, and wrong-doing, but very little attention is given to the lower profile companies who have basically abandoned their customers, other than to take their money.

I had a difficult time deciding where to put this example. Do I put it in the political chapter with the SEC, the Department of Justice, and the IRS? Do I put it in the judicial and legal chapter? It could really be an excellent example of dodging accountability in so many areas it is difficult to choose.

We had a local company by the name of Metropolitan Mortgage and Securities Company which had grown into a two-billion-plus dollar company. It was a second generation company, significant because of the trust component. The company met its demise via bankruptcy in 2004. It had thousands of investors, including a very large population of retirees whose life savings were tied up in the company. Needless to say, many people had their lives ruined by what was termed an "accounting scandal." The end result was that investors lost more than $600 million.

C. Paul Sandifur, Jr., the chairman and CEO and son of the founder, paid $150,000 to settle fraud allegations made by the U.S. Securities and Exchange Commission, plus $23,000 as part of a class action settlement. He was never charged with a crime. Four other former executives also agreed to pay a total of $45,000. One former president was convicted by a federal jury of lying to auditors. In total the settlement and SEC total would be $218,000. This money was then folded into a $38 million settlement with the major accounting firms and others involved. The settlements included NO ADMISSSION OF WRONG DOING.

I find it difficult to believe that all of the executives and the board were operating in a vacuum of knowledge. Lawyer's fees in cases such as these range from 25 to 33 per cent of the total. Once again, the lawyers, not the victims, are the big winners. You can do the math, but it was estimated that some investors would receive between 16 and 20 cents on the dollar. Most of the executives involved, including the CEO, were never charged criminally and apparently there was no insurance or bonding involved. What happened to fiduciary responsibility? The bottom line: NO Real Accountability!

By definition, free enterprise is an economic system in which private business operates in a competitive environment and is largely free of government control. But does this imply that there is no need for accountability in the system? Because of the competitive environment component it has been determined that there is a need for government intervention when there is a chance of lessening of competition, creating some accountability. There is a recent case where this very scenario has been played out, much to the detriment of several thousand people and their families.

Let me identify the villains in this story right up front. First is the Federal Trade Commission, the government agency tasked with enforcing accountability. Next is Comvest Partners, a private equity company, A.K.A. Haggen Foods. The story begins with a $9.4 billion merger of Albertsons and Safeway food companies. In its infinite bureaucratic wisdom the FTC issued an order that for the merger to

*Free Pass*

happen, Albertsons and Safeway had to sell off or divest themselves of 146 stores. Not 145 or 147, but 146. This must entail some secret mathematical formula.

The unfortunate problem is that the FTC's math does not take into account the 11,000 employees and their families who are involved. The reality: the FTC has impunity from accountability. They can make and reverse decisions with no concern for the people directly involved and with no real consequences for their actions. This is where Comvest Partners (Haggen Foods) slithers into the scene set up by the FTC.

Haggen Foods was a small grocery retailer with 18 stores headquartered in Bellingham, Washington. As a result of the FTC order, they were presented with the opportunity to acquire 146 of the Safeway and Albertsons stores. Sounds like a normal business transaction at this point, right? The problem is, as reported by the Seattle Times, the capital needed for the acquisition was raised by flipping real estate within the same timeframe as the acquisition was in process and announced. This is a commonplace tactic by private-equity firms and can raise millions of dollars very quickly, while at the same time reducing their risk in the acquisition. It is slick and legal under the current government rules and policies, but it is void of any protection for the employees involved.

In the span of nine months, the FTC issued an order to divest stores to accommodate a large merger, a private equity firm took advantage of this order to purchase 146 stores, mostly by flipping real estate, and then declared bankruptcy. I am certainly not a Wall Street expert, but I did spend a large part of my career working on mergers and acquisitions and even I could see the writing on the wall when it came to this deal. This entire sordid mess was virtually doomed from the outset, due to various factors, but the real victims and losers are the employees and their families and the communities that support them. Quite simply, they became pawns in a series of real estate transactions that profited a few. Unfortunately, there is no accountability for what they have been put through due to corporate greed. Coincidentally, the FTC has since reversed itself and is now allowing Safeway and Albertsons to reacquire some of the divested stores. There must have been a flaw in their original secret formula.

Since we are on the issue of corporate accountability, how about the tobacco companies? I know they have lost some lawsuits, costing them some money and forcing them to put warnings on packages, but these questions have swirled around in my mind. Are all of the board directors, executives and senior managers smokers, and are they required to smoke? If they don't smoke, why not? Do they encourage their spouses and children to smoke, when their children reach legal age, and if not, why? At their annual Christmas and Thanksgiving dinner, does the family sit around the table after dinner and light up?

*Free Pass*

My opinion is that Wall Street is a main perpetrator when it comes to a lot of corporations going off course and perhaps doing things and taking shortcuts that are not appropriate and sometimes Illegal. The pressure from Wall Street is immense to not only maintain stock value, but to grow wealth through stock appreciation. When is the last time you actually saw them held accountable for anything?

We want free enterprise and the entrepreneurial spirit to flourish and grow, but not without accountability.

# Chapter 5 - Justice for All Or Perhaps Just for Some

It is fair to state up front that we most likely live under the best justice system in the world. After saying that, pause for just a moment and think about a question. On a scale of one to five with five being very fair, equitable, consistent and effective, and one being the opposite, how would you rate our current justice system? Would that I could see your responses and have a dialogue as to why you answered the way you did.

As I was writing this particular chapter, we had an experience in my local community which brought home some shortcomings and questions concerning our system of justice, which includes the penal system. There were two sheriff's deputies who were shot and wounded while making a routine traffic stop. In this case, the alleged shooter was a convicted felon. There was not just a single conviction to his credit, but he had been arrested 25 times as an adult. The arrests led to convictions for drugs, burglary, theft, forgery, assault, driving under the influence and attempting to elude police. In 1997 the suspect fled a traffic stop and led a state trooper on a high-speed chase. The trooper injured his ribs and knees while struggling with the offender after the chase. The offender was then hospitalized for a possible drug overdose and then arrested on charges of resisting arrest, drug and gun possessions, and other charges.

Now some logical questions arise. Why is this individual out walking the streets? How much time and money do you suppose has been spent on the pursuit, arrest, temporary incarceration, hospitalization and trial of this one single individual? Regardless of how much it is, guess who paid for it? You and I, of course, not to mention the peace officers who were injured while dealing with him. I know the legal system and penal system is overwhelmed with individuals who have no character, no morals, no values and no apparent sense of right and wrong. But on the other hand, when does enough is enough come to bear?

How many times do you read about a child molester abusing a child, and in the story it is brought to light that he or she had been previously convicted of child molestation or rape, often times in multiple cases? It makes me sick to my stomach to think that another child has suffered because we as a society cannot figure out a way to put these animals in a place where they cannot harm our children.

It's time to rethink our priorities, our system and what we value. It's time for some rather radical thinking or rethinking about how we deal with criminals and the justice system in general. It is also critical that we rethink our judicial system, some certain laws, or lack thereof, and who the legal and penal system is really supposed to protect. I am weary of incompetent judges and the legislators who are soft on crime and dole out ridiculous sentencing guidelines. Their actions result in a revolving door for criminals. I am fed up with the extraordinary costs associated with supporting a broken system. I do not want to get rid of the fundamental precepts of the legal system. Things such as innocent until proven guilty, right to a speedy trial and the right to an attorney, among other things, should be preserved, but we need appropriate accountability and the consequences that go along with it.

I am not a huge proponent of the death penalty, but neither do I object to it. Let me offer you a scenario that does exemplify my frustrations and concerns, and where my thoughts lie. A criminal breaks into a home to rob a family; chances are great that he is a repeat offender. The adults awaken and go to check out the noise. The intruder is startled and shoots and kills one or both homeowners. Not too much of an unusual occurrence, wouldn't you agree? The intruder is captured and tried and hopefully convicted. Unless of course he gets off on a technicality. (Maybe one of the arresting officers had bad breath and the criminal's senses were violated.)

Let's assume he was convicted for the sake of our example. He broke into the home with the express intent of taking something that was not his. More than likely he is a drug user. More than likely he is a career criminal. More than likely he has never held a meaningful job nor attempted to even get one.

We, as taxpayers, paid for the officers and all costs associated with them. We paid for the trial. We paid for the public defender. We may even pay for an appeal; maybe the attorney found a technicality or loophole. Finally, he is convicted and sent to prison, probably for a paltry amount of time. Remember, the prisons are overcrowded. Regardless, we now pay for his room and board.

We pay for his full medical and dental. Because we are compassionate, (after all, he only killed two people while trying to take their personal possessions) we pay for his recreation. He gets to watch HD color television, work out in a gym and has access to the internet. Oh yeah, he still has access to drugs.

I was in China a number of years ago on business. One day we were driving down a street and I observed a very large and incredibly ominous building sitting prominently on top of a hill. It looked like something out of medieval times. The building was very stark and made of stone with walls probably fifty feet high. There were virtually no visible windows and it was depressing just to look at it. Thinking it might be an old castle or abandoned government building of some sort, I inquired of the driver what it was. He replied that it was a prison and that it was in use. I said that it was so large it must contain a great many prisoners. His response was that it was such a bad place that it was virtually empty. It seems that people wanted to avoid it and crime was virtually nonexistent.

Before you get your shorts in a knot, I am not even coming close to advocating a Chinese style of justice or penal system in this country. I am well aware of their civil and human rights violations. What I am asking you to consider is something in the middle. We are overwhelmed with crime and the associated costs in this country. We have gone from "and justice for all" and "provide for the common welfare" to a system that goes out of its way to protect and coddle the criminal element.

When looking at the court system, we might as well start at the top, with the highest court in the land, the site of last appeals, The Supreme Court of the United States. When there is a major issue garnering strong national attention, especially one with strong social and cultural implications, do you ever really expect a fair, unbiased, impartial, objective or non-political decision? Of course not. The court is mostly a politically motivated decision-making body. They are not about to go against the political ideology of the party of the president who appointed them. It is pretty much a foregone conclusion as to how the individual judges will render their decisions.

*Free Pass*

This group is, in theory, supposed to be the ultimate gatekeepers of justice and defenders of the Constitution. In fact, they are political appointees with jobs for life, and they are held above any accountability. It's rather amusing to listen to the media talk about a pending decision as if there is some possibility of a surprise, objective, and impartial decision.

To confirm my suspicions that the Supreme Court is politically biased and not objective, I went to the internet, and to Wikipedia specifically, since they seemed to have the most comprehensive and thorough body of research on the subject. To quote them, "It has long been commonly assumed that the votes of Supreme Court justices reflect their jurisprudential philosophies as well as their ideological leanings, personal attitudes, values, political philosophies, or policy preferences. A growing body of academic research has confirmed this understanding: scholars have found that the justices largely vote in consonance with their perceived values. Using statistical analysis of Supreme Court votes, scholars found that an inferred value representing a justice's ideological preference on a simple conservative-liberal scale is sufficient to predict a large number of that justice's votes." Is it any wonder that presidents are so eager to appoint Supreme Court justices? There is always that need on their part to stack the deck. They are not interested in justice, fairness or objectivity. They are only interested in perpetuating their philosophy, ideology and legacy.

*M. Randall Long*

I understand there will always be bias and prejudice on the part of any human being making decisions and passing down verdicts. My point is that Supreme Court justices are exempt from any accountability due to their lifetime appointments. The Constitution is not crystal clear on the issue of lifetime appointments, and it is high time the issue was visited because the court has become increasingly political.

The Attorney General of the United States, often referred to as the "Top Cop," is another political appointee who has probably outlived their credibility due to a lack of accountability, except to the person who appointed them. They are supposed to be the ultimate enforcer of the law and should operate at the highest level of trust. I am afraid that in today's political climate it is just simply not the case. They get to pick and choose what issues, problems and laws they will intervene in, and it seems they have become more concerned with the political implications and in pleasing the person who appointed them than in seeking truth and justice. Unfortunately, this is just an observation based on recent events, with no apparent way to substantiate it.

I can remember the days when I assumed the American Civil Liberties Union was a high-integrity defender of truth and justice, not some ideological purveyor of biased and slanted agendas. As a case in point of one of their agendas, I present the following example. They announced that they will try to provide top civilian defense attorneys for alleged

69

*Free Pass*

terrorists facing trial at Guantanamo Bay, Cuba -- including the alleged mastermind of the September 11, 2001 terrorist attacks. Former Attorney General Janet Reno is among the top lawyers who've endorsed the $8.5 million effort, which will help coordinate and defray the expenses of civilian defense attorneys working on the terrorism cases. Anthony Romero, ACLU Executive Director, said a major thrust of the effort will be to defend Khalid Sheik Mohammed. Officials say Khalid confessed to masterminding the September 11 attacks as well as several other terrorist acts, including the beheading in Pakistan of Wall Street Journal correspondent Daniel Pearl. I would assume that once the ACLU gets this resolved, they can proceed with the anti-defamation suit on behalf of Adolph Hitler. After all, he has probably not received the defense he deserves.

So many holes have developed, technicalities evolved, so much inept legislation and general incompetence in the system that it seems to be just a shell of what it was intended to be. My belief is that the proliferation of attorneys is one of the main culprits. One has only to glance at a daily newspaper, look online or watch a newscast to see what I mean.

We have a local infamous citizen whose name does not deserve to be mentioned. In the most recent account I found, he was rearrested after escaping from a correction facility. This may not be noteworthy, other than why he was allowed to escape. The real story is that his criminal history spans nearly three decades and includes at least 20 convictions, primarily for drug and property crimes. It has been estimated that he has cost the justice system over $1 million.

One of the areas in our justice system that really gets my attention is the incessant delay, promulgated by the attorneys and allowed by the judges. Some cases stretch from days to months to years. I can remember a local high profile case involving a police officer which I followed for almost two years. Yes, I said two years. Every time I thought there was going to be progress and a trial, the attorneys filed a motion for an extension or delay, which seemed to always be granted. Apparently they had to go interstellar in search of new evidence and data. The defendant was eventually convicted, which seemed he would be from the beginning, but he was kept out of prison for an extended period because of delays. Not only is this dodging accountability, but runs up an incredible tab on the taxpayers' dime.

A person's life seemingly has lost all value in our legal system, or at least has been greatly diminished. Take the case of a man in Seattle who was drinking and fell asleep while holding his seven-month-old son near a fire pit. The medical examiner stated that the baby died of smoke inhalation and burns on 100 percent of his body. Can you imagine the pain and suffering endured by this child? If convicted of second-degree manslaughter, he will face a standard sentence range of 21 to 27 months in prison. A baby is essentially tortured and killed and his life is worth less than three years? By the way, the father in question is an illegal immigrant who has been deported three times. If this example is not sufficient testimony, go back and review the case of the affluenza teen. The judge in that case said by his actions that the lives of four individuals carried no value.

The accountability and consequences for driving under the influence is another anomaly I simply cannot grasp. A typical DUI involves someone under the influence of alcohol or drugs, becoming impaired and getting behind the wheel of a potentially lethal weapon. It happens on a routine basis -- almost daily. But the situations that gain our attention are in those instances when we see someone killed by a drunk driver and it is revealed it is not their first offense. Oftentimes, they have multiple offenses.

My state's legislature, with the signature of the governor, just signed a bill that will double the maximum fine and prison sentence for a felony-level DUI conviction. Double is the defining word, and apparently something to be celebrated as an accomplishment. The travesty is that under the new law, a person's fifth DUI within 10 years is a felony, but the first four are gross misdemeanors. A DUI for someone previously convicted of vehicular assault or vehicular homicide while intoxicated is also a felony-level offense. Now this is a law we can all be proud of, especially those who lose loved ones to a drunk driver: a drunk driver who only has three convictions.

We have watered down, removed, and distorted accountability in the justice system to the point that it is only a shell of what it could and should be. Criminals are now in a position to thumb their noses at the system, knowing that a crafty attorney can work the system, impose delays and find loopholes in laws to their client's advantage and to the disadvantage of the law-abiding citizens. I live in an area that experiences one of the highest car theft rates in the country. If you ask the local police, they will tell you that car thieves are released from the system faster than they can be put in. Most of them are repeat offenders.

I have a personal situation that clearly brought into focus what actually happens in the so-called justice system. A few years ago I, along with several other victims, was involved locally with the manager of a real estate escrow company who embezzled money from us. My loss amounted to almost $25,000. Of course we all assumed that we were protected by insurance and bonding. Not so fast! The insurance company refused to pay off based on some technicality. The manager who embezzled the funds had committed suicide, which somehow affected the coverage. I hired an attorney to represent me and was on a contingency agreement at about 37% of what she would recover.

I quickly discovered that the judges and attorneys in town are part of a good old boy network. For example, the judges routinely give all or at least most of the receivership and related cases to a certain attorney. A sweet deal, right? I found out right away that the court-appointed attorney couldn't care less about the victims and was more interested in taking care of his cronies in real estate and related areas. He did virtually nothing in the best interests of the victims, and actually seemed intent on taking care of the offender's family. Any semblance of fairness or justice was purely coincidental.

I filed a very detailed and thorough complaint with the State Bar Association. You can guess how that came out. My attorney eventually admitted that she was up against a brick wall and there was nothing else she could do. I was not satisfied with her conclusion, so I did my own research. I suggested that we file a lawsuit against the owners for lack of exercise of fiduciary responsibility. She wrote a letter to the owners and we had a check back within a week. Of course, 37% was deducted from my claim for doing my own legal work.

My faith and confidence in the legal system was crushed in the aforementioned case. I was naïve in my assumption that the system was there for our protection. Instead, I found out that there is a huge fraternity of lawyers and judges who primarily look out for each other. There are judges who look the other way, and who are not tough in their standards and expectations regarding the attorneys in their courtrooms. These same judges are willing contributors to delays and incessant continuances. I found that the victim has no real advocate when it comes to justice, oftentimes not even his own attorney.

I saw firsthand that insurance and bonding protection in financial matters can be a hollow promise. It seems the insurance companies have even more expensive lawyers who are skilled in finding ways to avoid paying claims. Perhaps my biggest disappointment is in the way judges hand out favoring status to the same attorneys when it comes to receiverships. The ones receiving the favors know they have no accountability and will be protected by the judge and the bar. Apparently the judges have no accountability when it comes to favoritism. I am hopeful my personal example is not the norm everywhere, but I would bet it is the case in too many areas.

Not to pick on the city near where I live, but it is such a fertile field to be plowed when it comes to the judicial and penal system. They go through police chiefs like people go through cheap socks, except cheap socks last a lot longer. The prosecutor's office and courts are equally inept. Take this latest example as proof. The case of an alleged serial killer has been pushed out months, if not over a year because of the resignation of three attorneys in the County Public Defender's Office. Why there are three attorneys on the case I will never understand, but so be it. They resigned because of an alleged ethics breach in the Defender's Office. This little fiasco will cost us hundreds of thousands of dollars. Character, professionalism and accountability seem to be lost terms in this little corner of justice.

*Free Pass*

If you think the number of lawyers in this country is growing exponentially, you are right. Thirty five years ago there were over 450,000 lawyers and the law schools were producing about 34,000 new ones each year. By 2011 there were over 1.22 million and 44,000 new ones added each year. According to the American Bar Association there were almost 1.4 million lawyers in 2015. To put it in perspective, 70% of the lawyers in the world reside in this country and there is roughly one lawyer per 763 people, including infants. The good news is that the number of lawyers in Congress is actually declining. That is surprising since I thought Congress was the solution for full employment for attorneys.

You may be asking what this has to do with accountability. I have several theories. With the huge amount of attorneys, it only stands to reason that it is in their best interest to make everything more complicated and more litigious. Why do you think attorneys gravitate toward elected offices? If they are successful in making things so complex and so difficult, it is job security for their brethren. If they advertise on radio, television, billboards and bus stop benches they can stimulate lawsuits, some of which are frivolous. Ask your doctor how much they have to pay for malpractice insurance and how much it affects your medical bills. Next time you buy or sell a home, look at how much paperwork you have to wade through.

I have come up with a video game. It is called The Scales of Justice. In the game you have a hypothetical legal issue and need an attorney to guide you through the legal system. To purchase the game you must read and sign a 75-page legal disclosure and release of liability, written so small it would be unreadable even with a high-powered microscope. It is highly recommended that you consult an attorney before signing.

You open a legal directory and have hundreds of choices. Of course you do not have the resources of the wealthy, so you must have an attorney who works on a contingency basis. You are already at a disadvantage, because the opposition has highly paid counsel and they can afford to stall and stonewall, and they happen to belong to the same country club as the judge. In short, they are going to make life so miserable you will want to quit. The opposition immediately puts you through the wringer. They subpoena all of your personal records, including your grade school transcripts. Everyone knows this is just an exercise to punish you and wear you down, but the judge supports it as discovery because he has known the other attorney since law school.

Next, the opposing attorney requests a delay of three months (he had an extended European vacation scheduled), plus it is a good tactic to wear you down and break down your will. Justice is not always about discovering the truth; rather it is oftentimes about a war of wills. Of course the judge concurs regarding the delay (their kids play soccer together). After several months of sheer terror and constant harassment, you prevail at level one. The opposition files an appeal, so no payout. You progress through two levels of appeal, taking a toll on your time, finances, psyche, and emotions. You finally reach the top level of the game, the Supreme Court, only to lose. You forgot one thing: the opposition voted for the right party, the party which controls the court. If it is any consolation, you only lost 60-70% of what you were entitled to.

The justice system is not a level playing field and there are a lot of lawyers who are not really interested in the truth and in justice. Their primary concern is to eliminate or at least minimize any financial accountability for their clients. If you think my game is an exaggeration and that there is a fair and equitable system, I have another real life example for your consideration.

I have two longtime and very close friends who are also small business owners. They have owned and operated family businesses for a very long time. There are two other things you need to know about them. They are people who are honest and have unimpeachable / character. In addition, they have both been suffering from some very severe illnesses for quite some time, predating their legal struggles. They own two retail businesses selling manufactured homes, one of which is adjacent to a rail yard and a chemical storage area. Magnesium chloride, a deicer, is transferred from railcars to the storage tanks at this location. My friends have experienced three different events where the material leaked onto their sales site. The first time, they elected to do nothing other than contact the company.

The president came out personally and assured them it would not happen again. Instead, it did happen again, twice. On at least one of the occasions it killed landscape vegetation on their site and was so bad they had to close their business for three weeks, during their peak selling season. The material ran under their sales office, accumulating to the point that it was causing headaches and extreme discomfort. It was so bad that the fire department had to be called to wash the area down. They were forced to file a lawsuit due to the lack of adequate response from the corporation.

The corporate attorneys representing the offending company, as well as the attorneys representing the company's insurance, proceeded to make life as miserable as possible for my friends. For example, they required payroll records back 20 years. They asked other inane questions such as how many firemen were there and what did they wear? The process resulted in a stack of depositions and documents over a foot tall. The corporate attorneys were vicious in their attacks of my friends and their family and employees, apparently in an attempt to wear them down and get them to surrender.

Needless to say, my friends are disillusioned when it comes to the justice system, even regarding their own attorney. To you and me, this would seem so logical, and the accountability so easy to determine. A chemical leaked onto an adjoining business at least three times, resulting in a response from the fire department. It killed the landscape vegetation, was messy and smelly to the point that it caused headaches and resulted in the closure of business for three weeks. Why could the company and their insurance not accept accountability and just do the right thing? Instead, as usual, the attorneys were the real winners. This process took over two years and justice was not served because the company and the insurance company want to dodge accountability at the physical and mental expense of the victims.

We all want the truth, and ultimately justice. But above all else we want accountability in the system and a level field. The nonsense, harassment, antagonism and endless delays need to be addressed. Judges need to stop the cronyism and use logic and fairness to both sides of an issue. My confidence in the legal system is at an all-time low. I am like a lot of others who believe the system is rigged, bogged down with ridiculous nonsense, unfair in a lot of cases, and corrupt in others. Of course, there is very little accountability to those tasked with ensuring fair and honest accountability.

# Chapter 6 - Entertainment and Sports Elite
# A Monster Has Been Created

The best thing about writing a book is that you get to ask yourself and others some questions that have plagued average people all our lives. One of the ones I am curious about and continue to be perplexed by is the red carpet.

"Hey, let's lay out a strip of red carpet and let a large group of arrogant, self-absorbed, wealthy, and narcissistic individuals walk down it."

Which enlightened individual said that? Hollywood, and New York even, do not have enough ego-maniacs and individuals starved for attention; we have to create a special high-profile venue to allow them to preen and pose for the cameras and media. Of course the commoners can only admire them in awe from an appropriate distance. After all, we only pay

*Free Pass*

$15 for a movie ticket and then a small ransom for a bag of popcorn (with genuine simulated butter) and a soft drink. It is actually closer to a year's wages in some third world countries.

I really do not begrudge anyone who is talented, shrewd and resourceful enough to take advantage of a system that allows them to make a lot of money off of everyday people who are willing to pay for a fantasy. But really, a red carpet? When they create a red carpet treatment for teachers, firemen, paramedics, the military, and policemen, count me in. I will gladly line up with my camera and adoration. But I reserve that kind of respect for those who really deserve it: those whose character and moral and ethical fiber deserve attention, and those who embrace accountability and command respect.

Granted, the red carpet does not have much of a direct correlation to a lack of accountability, but it does serve as a very visible and tangible example of the extreme and creative /measures the entertainment industry uses to set itself above the rest of society and thereby exempt itself from any sense of accountability. I would love to see some humility, and heaven forbid, some accountability from those who entertain us.

The entertainment industry — movies, television, and music — is by nature a master of marketing, self-promotion and self-aggrandizement. Performing artists and their producers have adeptly created the illusion that they are something very special and above the ordinary common people who create their wealth and fame. They have adroitly spun this impenetrable cocoon around themselves, their industry, and culture. The entertainment industry is a cesspool of greed, immorality, inflated egos, and corruption, all fed by drugs and alcohol. The worst part is that they exert extraordinary influence over us and especially over our children. Even our politicians, including the president, routinely make trips to Hollywood to tap into the vast reservoir of campaign dollars available.

Some of the Hollywood elite do not bother to stop with using their art to influence. They feel compelled to go to extraordinary lengths to peddle their distorted, biased and oftentimes destructive view of the world. Because of their status and position, they seek to influence public opinion and social values. Take Jane Fonda for example. She was a fairly good actress, I suppose, but not someone whom I want lecturing about foreign policy. Somehow I just don't think she is qualified. Even if she disagreed with the war in Viet Nam, which a lot of people did, she did not have the right to aid and abet the enemy to make her point. A lot of American men and women died at the hands of those whom she chose to support by her actions. In most circles she would be deemed a traitor, but in the Hollywood circles she is just another spoiled and privileged aristocrat who can do anything she wants without repercussions. The list in tinsel town seems endless, with extremists who want to influence the thinking of everyone, especially our youth. People like Michael Moore and Quentin

*Free Pass*

Tarantino and others strive to bend the thoughts and actions of young people to their way of thinking. It wouldn't be so bad if they used their power and influence in a balanced way and on societal issues where the influence might be helpful, but it all seems tilted in one direction: toward the political issues which most influence and help their own personal lifestyles and culture. Perhaps that is why so many politicians gravitate to the west coast when they are in need of money for campaign financing. The old adage, "You scratch my back and I'll scratch yours," seems to be the order of the day in the entertainment industry.

Television has often been referred to as a vast wasteland. In today's environment that would seem to be a dramatic understatement. I don't think of myself as an intellectual snob; in fact, I enjoy bubblegum for the mind as well as the next person. But give me a break. Keeping Up With the Kardashians? Are there actually that many people out there who can't think of anything better to do with their time and energy than to waste it enabling these types of individuals? I know the producers and networks couldn't care less, but surely intelligent and responsible people can hold these idiots accountable and not support a dysfunctional, immoral and arrogant group of people with no real talent or purpose. I dare not even mention the program Catlin, lest I be branded a bigot. It seems the hidden agenda is to dumb down the intellect and thinking of the viewing public, especially our children.

If insulting our intelligence was the only problem it would be bad enough, but it seems the entertainment industry has taken a particular aim at the youth of this country. Take the television show, Sex in the City. Not only was its title and content detrimental, but it appears that it also had an additional subversive agenda. It was portrayed as being cool by one of the lead actresses to smoke. It was widely acknowledged that the program encouraged a great many young girls to take up smoking. The actress, of course, couldn't care less if she influenced this behavior; she knew there was money involved, and of course no accountability. The producers and directors dismissed it as collateral damage.

How many times have you picked up a newspaper or magazine, read on the internet or saw on television, a story about someone in the entertainment industry who has gone to rehab, committed suicide, died of an overdose or disclosed an STD? There have been countless articles and stories chronicling the rampant drug use by entertainers. My question is, do the law enforcement agencies turn a deaf ear or a blind eye to the celebrities? Is there too much money involved, or is there too much pressure to leave it alone? Oh yeah, the politicians go there for funding. If you think it's just my own imagination, let me offer some quotes:

"Hollywood was notorious for its nonchalantly open use of the drug (cocaine) by celebrities." — Michael Kilian

"A knowledgeable studio executive tells Parade Magazine in 1996 that drug use is as big ... or bigger...than ever in the movie capitol." — Walter Scott

"Half the people in Hollywood seem to have gone through recovery from drugs and alcohol by now." — Roger Ebert

"A sort of heroin-cocaine chic exists in today's Hollywood." — Michael Wilmington

"During the freewheeling '70s, Hollywood seemed to be riding a coke-induced high. On screen, recreational drugs were the props of glamorous...or they were psychedelic aids in the search for Truth...Off-screen, drugs were part of the Hollywood mystique, seemingly taken as casually as a cocktail. Business deals were cut over vials of cocaine." — Jorge Casuso

If the knowledge is so available and obvious, who is giving out the free passes? And isn't it refreshing to know that when you go to a movie or concert, or tune in a television show you might be helping to fund a drug cartel?

Our latest Hollywood hero, Sean Penn, (you might remember that he is the one who was accused of punching a reporter), has decided he is not only an actor and activist, but is now qualified to be a journalist. By the way, I have always thought I might be a good surgeon; maybe he has motivated me to give it a try. Anyway, in his new role as a renowned journalist, he has been granted access to the Mexican drug lord El Chapo for an interview. Now this is not only ironic, from a Hollywood standpoint, but is also a bit disturbing. It raises interesting questions that allow one to fill in all kinds of speculative answers. First and foremost, why and how would someone of Sean Penn's ilk be granted an exclusive interview with one of the most notorious drug lords in the world -- the very guy who might supply drugs in copious amounts to the entertainment industry? I know I routinely turn to Rolling Stone magazine for the hard-hitting, objective and trustworthy journalism I depend on. Just another example of the Hollywood elite having access, influence and no accountability. The list of issues and bad actors (no pun intended) in the entertainment industry could fill an entire book, or maybe an anthology, but I will leave it at that.

Let me make a disclaimer before I delve into the world of sports, and primarily professional athletics. As a kid I played sports and loved games of all kinds, maybe due in part to my competitive nature. I continued my love of sports into my adulthood and followed them closely. Some of my earliest heroes were athletes, people like Mickey Mantle, YA Tittle, and Don Merideth. In the last few years my excitement, enthusiasm and respect for the world of sports has greatly diminished. Part of it is not even related to a lack of accountability, but rather other factors. I have trouble staying interested in teams composed of mercenaries. I also have trouble maintaining an interest in teams where wealthy owners are on one side and wealthy players are on the other. Two competing sides of millionaires, paid for by everyday Joes, just doesn't appeal to me anymore. Occasionally I will turn on professional football or baseball, but rarely do I watch an entire game. I do still enjoy college sports, but even have some issues there.

My growing disenchantment with professional teams stems mostly from the blatant lack of accountability and the arrogance associated with such disregard. To put the situation in context, we have to recognize a couple of facts. First, professional athletes are not really any different than the Hollywood crowd: they are entertainers. Secondly, like Hollywood, it's all about money; in fact, it's just big business. As such, the dollars and cents take precedence over all else. If a professional athlete is involved in a brawl, knife fight, gun play or other offense at 3:00 in the morning, they instantly dodge accountability. Chances are good that if their own team happens to impose any consequences (but probably not), the next team they play for will be ready and willing to forgive, forget, and ring up the cash register. Now if you and I were to get in trouble at 3:00 in the morning at a night club, do you think there would be any accountability and consequences from our employer?

To fund these millionaire owners and players requires a tremendous amount of cash. The average major league baseball salary is more than four million. The average professional basketball salary is 5.15 million, and the average professional football salary is 1.9 million. Where does this cash come from? There is of course television, and we all know where they get their revenue. Then there are the games themselves. Ticket prices are astronomical, plus parking, and of course there are the $10 hotdogs and $20 beers. Ask a middle-class dad if he can afford to take his family to a professional football game. Those poor babies in the NFL are the lowest paid on the professional sports ladder. I'm not sure how they scrape by on that paltry amount. I do know that they are quick to point out that the professional longevity of their careers is relatively short, but how long would it take you and me to earn $1.9 million? It's all just a part of the professional sports propaganda.

The athletic elite are similar to the Hollywood entertainment elite in that they have done a masterful job of setting themselves apart from and above any accountability. I recognize there are probably some professional sports owners who adhere to strict values, standards and expectations, but there are a great many who seemingly do not. The bottom line dollars appears to remove any sense of accountability. The substance abusers, wife beaters and other assorted felons just seem to rotate among the teams who have a need to fill a position on their team. All you have to do is go through the rosters and see how many players have had suspensions for substance abuse or felonies.

*Free Pass*

Why should we be concerned? Who do your children hold up as heroes and role models? Who do your kids emulate? Whose name is on the souvenir jersey they buy and wear? Is it one belonging to a convicted abuser or other felon, or even an accused performance enhancing drug user?

It is incomprehensible to me why someone who is gifted, wealthy and famous has to resort to drugs, excessive alcohol use, and generally bad behavior. There is a seemingly endless list of professional athletes who cannot or will not stay out of trouble. That same list is laced with individuals who want to get in trouble, but dodge any form of accountability.

The music industry has slowly but surely been sinking into the quicksand of vile, angry, destructive and malicious content. The music industry as a whole and a significant number who perform in it have sunk to new lows in societal values. They do this (apparently) for the sake of money, fame, notoriety, and competition to outdo their rivals. We now have unusually young singers and musicians who have decided they have no limits to their ridiculous behavior off the stage. Some are even the children of well-known entertainers. This speaks volumes to the lack of parental involvement in the character development of their offspring. It is difficult to determine just how much of the bad behavior is of their own volition and how much is suggested by their publicist because it just seems to influence our young people to buy more of their records and follow their every move. It is truly regrettable that these individuals have been set up as role models.

I understand that drugs and alcohol have been a part of the entertainment culture for as long as any of us care to remember, but it seems to be growing at an ever-increasing rate. Television is even quick to capitalize by taking the spouses of the known drug abusers in the music business and showcasing them, giving further credibility to the problem.

I'm not sure how there can be such widespread knowledge of the issues in the entertainment business without any accompanying accountability. Virtually everyone in America is aware of the fact that a huge segment of the celebrity population uses and abuses drugs. It seems that there is a story all too frequently of an entertainer who has overdosed on drugs, and to top it off, those closest to him or her acknowledged the problem after the fact. Who is protecting the celebrities, and why are they being protected? One has to wonder just where one goes to get the free pass?

Perhaps Roman Polanski personifies the Hollywood and celebrity mindset and culture better than any other. Polanski is a film director, producer, writer and actor. He is obviously a very talented guy in the performing arts arena, but not so much when it comes to character and morals. In 1977 he was arrested for the rape of a 13-year-old girl. Yes, I said that correctly: she was 13 years old. He pled guilty to the charge of statutory rape and served 42 days in prison before being released.

*Free Pass*

He then fled to Paris before sentencing. I suppose it was, and maybe still is, easy for high profile celebrities, while awaiting sentencing, to casually board airplanes headed out of the country. I am not certain you or I could do it. He chose to dodge accountability due to his Hollywood celebrity status, but other factors give you a glimpse into the culture and attitude. First, many Hollywood executives came to his defense. After all, what can be the emotional and physical harm to a 13-year-old girl? The most astonishing thing is what has happened in the succeeding years. The Academy has bestowed numerous awards upon his work while he is in exile. He may be a convicted felon hiding out from justice, but come on, he makes a hell of a film, and they love him. Hollywood has issued yet another free pass from accountability.

It is ironic that the entertainers love to issue scathing political and cultural commentary on politics, what is politically correct and societal issues in general, but seem oblivious to the sordid mess that exists all around them. They love accountability when it comes to others who they disagree with, but loath it when applied to their own culture and industry. I believe they call that hypocrisy.

# Chapter 7 - Education
# We Have an Equation
# That Needs Solving

The memory is in my mind as if it happened only yesterday. It was one of those significant life experiences that is indelibly imprinted in my memory. As a sophomore in high school I was sitting in algebra class. Math was not my forte, to say the least. I studied hard, but struggled. A funny quip really applied to me and my math prowess: "I was very good at math until the alphabet decided to get involved." The math teacher called me up to the board to work a problem. She may as well have called me up to sit in the electric chair. Fear and dread gripped me as I walked to the chalkboard. You might remember the black or green boards and the white chalk sticks. Just the walk up to the board seemed to be in slow motion, as I anticipated the humiliation that was to follow.

*Free Pass*

I was totally lost trying to solve the equation. I wanted to be anywhere at that moment, other than at that board. Finally the teacher, and I use that term loosely, determined that it was not within my ability to solve the question. A good instructor might have said and done any number of things, none of which were said by her. I can still hear her words ringing in my ears when she said, "I am really glad that I have students like Randy … I need someone to pick up my trash."

Of course there is nothing quite so demeaning, so humiliating, and so embarrassing as to fail in front of your peers, but to have the teacher say such things is inexcusable. Now some might say she was trying to motivate me, but I can assure you she had no such intent. She was an awful educator with a mean spirit, and should not have been allowed in the classroom. She had never really been held accountable for her instructional abilities, or lack thereof. She knew that regardless of her words or actions there would be no consequences.

In a similar, and first hand vein, my youngest son experienced a teacher who probably should not have had a teaching certificate, at least based on what I know. My son is gifted academically and especially so in math and science. No, he obviously did not inherit my math genes; he consistently made A's in all of his math and science classes, with perfect scores in his AP (Advanced Placement) classes, including calculus. That is, until his physics AP Class. He scored a three, which was totally out of character. I was suspicious, and questioned him about why. He told me that a great deal of the material was not covered in class. Thinking that I was a biased and overly protective parent, I spoke with some of his classmates. They affirmed what he had told me. Upon further investigation I found out that the physics teacher was regarded as an extremely poor instructor, and was glaringly complacent, but had been with the district a long time, and is also a sports official. The bottom line is he is viewed as untouchable, and therefore immune from accountability.

Before you draw the wrong conclusion, this is absolutely not an attack on teachers. Far from it. As a matter of fact, you will be hard-pressed to find anyone more supportive of educators than me. They have my highest level of respect and admiration. They are probably the most poorly paid and underappreciated group of professionals around. My point is that all educators are not created equal. The vast majority of teachers are committed, dedicated, caring and competent. But there are also those, as reflected above, who are not fit to be in the classroom. They are coasters, slackers and game players, who are either incompetent, uncaring, or both. The problem is they are teaching our children.

If you ask a principal, one who will speak the truth, they will tell you the reality. It is essentially impossible to terminate a poorly performing teacher. Rather, what happens is that the poor performer is transferred to another school and it becomes their problem until a sufficient amount of time has passed and they can transfer him or her to another school. It becomes a game of passing the problem.

I am a strong proponent of the traditional bell curve. There are some truly exceptional, highly motivated, and gifted professionals. There is also a huge group of teachers in the middle — those who work hard, care about the kids and demonstrate classroom skills on a daily basis. But the fact is, there is a group of poor performers out on the edge. But guess what: that group of outstanding performers is paid exactly the same amount as the average performer and the same as those poor performers, assuming the same tenure and degree level. Is this really an incentive for superior performance, and a reason to create accountability in the education system? I understand how this pattern of ignoring accountability has evolved through union contracts, but it does not help the overall goal and incentivizing of academic excellence and of creating an environment of accountability.

We need a system of pay for performance in the public education world, and I believe the problems surrounding the perception of fairness can be resolved. As in most other professions, I would venture a guess that the teachers, and especially the union, believes that the evaluating authority, the principal, cannot be fair and objective. Therefore, the default logic is that you treat everyone equally and assume that everyone performs up to the same standard. Of course we all know that is flawed thinking.

Nonetheless, accountability surrounding performance has been all but eliminated, both good and bad. We must put accountability back into the classroom if we are going to compete in the world economy. We must also recognize and reward exceptional teachers with incentive-based pay.

Even though I worked in a rather large school district for two years as Director of Human Resources and had a large dose of firsthand experience, I decided that it might be interesting and enlightening to actually work in the classroom. I therefore signed on to become a substitute teacher at a local school district. I wanted to see if some concerns I had were truly warranted.

One experience was not only eye opening and stunning, but was also a bit frightening. I encountered an elementary school student at one of my assignments who I will call Bud (not his real name, of course). Bud was in my fifth grade math class, along with about 25 other students.

The regular teacher had left me a very clear and definite lesson plan of what was to be accomplished. After introducing myself and taking attendance, I wrote the assigned work plan on the board and instructed the students to begin.

Very quickly I noticed that all of the students had begun to focus on the assigned tasks: all except one. Bud wore a hoodie and had his head on the desk. I walked over and asked why he was not working, and suggested that he do so.

He replied, "I don't want to."

Several members of the class chimed in at this point saying, "He never does any work, he just sits there."

I was stunned, and did not know whether to send him to the office or what to do exactly. I chose to just leave him alone, although I eventually sent him to the office for distracting and disrupting the class. He was not gone very long before he returned, and just sat there quietly with a smug grin on his face.

At the end of the day, I caught the principal and asked her what his situation was. She replied that no one really knew, and that a lot of time and effort had been put into figuring out what his problem was. She also told me that he was very capable and could do the work, but chose not to. She also said that he had been sent home on suspension numerous times, mostly for fighting. They had been dealing with him since the first grade.

I then asked the most obvious question, "Why has he not been held back?"

Her answer absolutely shocked and amazed me. She replied, "Students cannot be held back without the parents' permission."

When exactly did the parents become qualified to determine the academic achievement of their child? This raises so many questions it is ridiculous. Who allowed this to happen and why? Is this fair to the students who do the work and are legitimately promoted? But of course, in the context of this book, who is accountable?

In this case there is a whole list of people who are not being responsible. Of course Bud's parents are not taking responsibility. As a side note, another teacher told me that on the day of one of his suspensions she had seen Bud and his parents at a local amusement center, no doubt for some quality parenting and no acceptance of accountability. Where are the school district leadership and the school board? Why are they allowing this to happen?

My guess is that they are afraid of being sued. Someone, at some point, must take a firm stand and do the right thing. Quit pawning the problem off on the school, the principal, the teachers, and the other students. If I was making the decision, Bud would not be allowed back in class without a parent being there to supervise him. He also would be held back until he completed an acceptable level of accomplishment. I would also be willing to take on the attorney that will enter the scene to make a buck off the backs of the taxpayers.

My goal is not to make generalizations, and this is true for the following issue in public education. There appear to be a great many entrenched and elitist school administrations, also known as district administrators. In addition to some personal experiences, I have spoken to numerous parents, teachers and former teachers, all of whom reflect this same observation.

There is no wonder that distrust is rampant in some school districts. It is ironic that a great many district administrators hold themselves above the parents and population in general when it comes to expertise in education, yet the results do not reflect it.

I can vividly remember sitting across the table from an assistant superintendent while interviewing for the position of Human Resources Director. During the interview she asked me the question, "How would you deal with meddling parents who want to question things?" In too many cases this seems to be the mentality.

How many of you reading this book have a guaranteed lifetime appointment in your job? Are you immune from performance management standards, free to do what you choose and are essentially bulletproof? Welcome to the world of higher education and the tenured professor. Curious about how and why this ever came into being, I researched and found the answer. Apparently it started in 1158 with the Holy Roman Emperor Frederick Barbarossa. He issued an edict protecting scholars and their academic freedom. It soon spread worldwide, and later included higher education in the United States. Of course, it still persists today.

I am not sure what they need to be protected from in today's environment. Quite the contrary: we need protection from them. They are so sheltered and untouchable that they now have the license to say and do whatever they please, regardless of whether it is relevant to the subject matter they are supposed to be teaching.

They have an open stage and microphone to espouse any ideology, philosophy or platform that they choose, with no accountability. They can denounce any spiritual value, moral value, political view, social norm, or anything else that is on their minds. If my child is in a college chemistry class, what right does this wingnut have to criticize my son or daughter for their spiritual or moral values? Who deputized them as the cultural, social, spiritual, and political correctness police? They would be the first to scream bloody murder if the shoe was on the other foot. All of this freedom without any repudiation, consequences or accountability is unacceptable, especially in today's culture of upwardly spiraling education costs.

A significant number of them have decided that it is their job in life to not only educate the students in the subject matter they were hired to teach, but also in what they believe to be true in general. Most of them have been isolated in their academic world and have never held a significant job in business or industry.

Case in point: I graduated with a bachelor's degree, worked for a little over a year, was drafted into the military, and served four years. I returned and worked for two years, and decided to pursue a master's degree. I was about halfway through the program when I took a human resources class.

The professor was a young guy with a doctorate. It was obvious that he had probably gone straight through school — undergraduate, masters and doctorate — with very little, if any, real world experience. We were discussing salaried compensation and salaried compensation systems one evening when he made an almost unbelievable statement. "Companies should take all of the mystery and intrigue out of compensation and just simply post everyone's salary on the board for all to see."

I sat there in silence as long as I could, and then asked a question. "That is a very interesting premise, how much do you make?" There was complete and total silence in the room as a failing grade flashed before my eyes.

He retorted, "Not enough."

I then asked, "You are advocating a compensation philosophy and program. Why don't you go ahead and model it for the class and tell us how much you make?"

Again there was stunned silence, his face turned red, and he finally responded. "Point well made, Mr. Long."

He had no real experience, yet he was teaching a class based on his personal philosophy and bias. He was teaching a point contradictory to reality and employee confidentiality, and certainly not a point he was willing to apply personally.

There is another key piece in higher education that seems to have escaped any true scrutiny and accountability. Perhaps my concerns are unwarranted, but based on my own observations it seems so.

First, one has to begin with the fact that college professors must write and publish and/or do research. This usually results in publication of the findings. In order to carry out this research, the professor must write and apply for grants: sometimes from private funds, but more often from the Department of Education or other federal sources.

I personally know of two professors, husband and wife, who have never worked in a job outside academia. They went straight through higher education, including a doctorate, and went right to work in a university. They both live off the grant process, meaning their income is solely dependent on their research grants, which translates to tax dollars in most cases. I have listened to them discuss their research and what if any impact it has on anything. I walked away shaking my head.

If you look at the political chapter and the frivolous spending and waste, you can make the connection. I am totally in favor of research and the contribution it makes ... assuming it is valid, productive and useful. My problem is that there seems to be little, if any, accountability for results and added value from the research. It seems to be an endless cycle of applying, funding and starting over, with no measurement of results or benefit. Who is accountable?

There are some facts about our public education system that are frightening. Thirty years ago America was the leader in quantity and quality of high school diplomas. Today the United States is 36th worldwide. Whenever one goes from a leader in any endeavor to being mediocre at best it becomes a major concern, especially in an area so critical as education. Teacher quality is one of the most significant factors related to student achievement. In the U.S., 14% of new teachers resign by the end of their first year of teaching, 33% resign within the first 3 years and 50% quit by their fifth year. This statistic seems very relevant to the decline in achievement spotlighted above, but is also a key factor in the present potential crisis in education, which is an acute teacher shortage. We must solve the issues of shortage and quality while building accountability.

High schools are not preparing students with the skills and knowledge necessary to excel after graduation. Only one in four high school students graduates college-ready in the four core subjects of English, math, reading, and science. In addition, 66% of all U.S. fourth grade students in America scored "Below Proficient" on the 2013 National Assessment of Educational Progress Reading Test, meaning they are not reading at grade level. Those with a low-income background number 80% below proficient, which indicates we are really failing our children in low income neighborhoods. Let me state here, college is not the answer for everyone. We must have our kids "Job Ready" in some capacity.

In 2012, in an analysis of student performance on the Programme For International Student Assessment, the United States placed 27th out of 34 countries in math performance and 20th in science performance.

*M. Randall Long*

In 2010, the federal government--the Department of Education specifically--came out with something called the Common Core. It was an attempt by the government to come up with a common curriculum, or what they thought would put our country back on track toward academic excellence and improve our standing on the international education stage. All states bought into it with the exception of Alaska, Nebraska, Texas, and Virginia. The price for not buying in or not adopting it: potential loss of federal funding via educational grants from the Department of Education.

Historically, the American tradition when it comes to education has been one of favoring decentralized control (in other words, a right of the states), and decentralized funding (most of us fund education through our property taxes, state lotteries and other forms of local and state taxes). Common Core has been controversial; to say the least, but a great many experts, including parents and educators, think it is a major step back. Based on recent data surrounding achievement and international standing, they would seem to be right.

Count me as one of those who do not believe the federal bureaucracy has any competence in determining a national public education curriculum. These are the same people who cannot or will not clean up waste and frivolous spending. Are we going to put them in charge of our children's educational future?

*Free Pass*

One final observation, and perhaps a question, about the current environment in public education is relevant. Do the kids really need to bring cell phones to class, and more often than not, be allowed to listen to music while working or testing? How can a teacher possibly monitor what the student is actually listening to or looking at? I have considered both sides of the argument, but do not see how turning on an electronic device in class is appropriate or enhance the learning experience.

We have been talking about improving education, the decline in educational excellence, and student achievement in this country for a long time, and apparently with little result. Who do we hold accountable? State superintendents and state boards, local superintendents and school boards, teachers, or parents? Who can fix it? I believe it is all of the above, working together to figure out what the problems are and then coming up with a plan, including a component centered on accountability.

The educational deficiencies in this country are not something that would be nice to fix. The deficiencies must be fixed, and soon, if we are going to compete in the global economy.

Fixing the problem starts with accountability.

# Chapter 8 - Et Cetera
# The Story With
# No Apparent Ending

It seems that the lack of accountability is a never-ending story. Just as I finish a chapter, something new pops up or there is a sequel to a story I have cited. The unfortunate truth is that even I am surprised by the depth and breadth of the lack of accountability. It seems so pervasive and in so many nooks and crannies of our everyday lives and society, that we take it for granted and accept it as the norm. For the most part we have become apathetic and conditioned to accept it.

What is the biggest rip-off? You are invited to choose one or all of the following options:

1. Razor Blades - they must be made out of a rare metal found only on certain asteroids. Do you ever actually see them on sale, at least at a significant savings? No, instead they offer you a can of shaving cream, worth maybe 50 cents, their cost. To combat this legalized

crime I have joined one of the on-line shaving clubs. I now pay a fraction of the price for a blade.

2. Printer Ink Cartridges - obviously a teaspoon of this magical elixir contains the distilled sweat of the rare and elusive golden hummingbird. It seems that on my printer I can replace the ink cartridge, print 10 pages and then get the message that my ink may be running low. Basically a ruse to convince me to go out and buy more ink. Inside the cheap plastic housing there must be an eyedropper of this rare and precious commodity.

3. Maintenance work done at the dealership - based on the hourly rate, the mechanics, I mean technicians, must be sent abroad to study and ultimately receive a doctorate in automotive technology. Of course the auto makers are involved in this elaborate scheme. Their goal is to build a car that is increasingly difficult to work on and that requires increasingly more expensive parts, and the labor to replace those parts.

4. Cable companies - we discussed these rip-off con artists in the corporate chapter, but they are basically an unregulated, or so it seems, monopoly that continues to take advantage of the public with higher bills, poor service and dictatorial business practices.

5. The big pharmaceutical companies - they do some amazing things, but are also master gougers and manipulators with no real accountability. If the doctor says you need this particular drug, what are your alternatives? Some drugs go way beyond the realm of

reasonableness based on price. There are people who must make choices between a drug and having food on the table. The drug companies' co-conspirators are...

6. The health insurance companies - the insurance company's main goal in life seems to be to take in the maximum amount of premiums, but give out the barest minimum in claims. This includes Medicare.

7. The energy sector - we all know about "big oil" and their credibility level, but the real and most relevant story is told at the gas pump of your local service station. We have been experiencing a welcome decline in fuel prices this past year, but it has been a catalyst for me to really pay attention to what is going on. I happen to drive by several gas stations in my daily travels, and have noticed some remarkable things. When crude oil prices are falling, prices at the pump have a significant lag. The Chevron station in my neighborhood sometimes takes weeks to reflect the change. But now that crude prices are trending up, the price at the pump moves up seemingly hourly. It is almost as if they have their hand on the price switch when it goes up. Do you think there is any accountability anywhere? We are so conditioned, that everyone in this sector just plays us. After all, they are all in lockstep. If I was the suspicious type, I might think there is collusion. Naw, we know we can trust the oil companies, right?

8. The precious metals market - much like the energy sector, it seems obvious that there is manipulation, collusion and other artificial

market influencers. This is another example of behind-the-scenes control from unknown and unnamed sources. Definitely not a free market system, and certainly one free from accountability.

9. Retail - why do I have to go in to a store to purchase something, only to get to the counter to pay for something or to get assistance and the telephone rings? The sales person answers the phone and then proceeds to help the person who chose to call in versus me, who took the time and effort to make a personal appearance.

And now for some post scripts...

Last night I started to shut down my computer to go to bed and guess what? I was greeted by a message on my screen that said, "Do Not Unplug or Turn Off Your Computer. Installing 14 updates." This morning I turned on my computer, knowing it would have to configure the updates from last night before I could use it. When I started to shut it down to rush to a meeting, I got another message. "Do Not Unplug or Turn off Your Computer. Installing 4 updates." Now I ask you, is there a big room filled with geeks with pocket protectors and black-rimmed glasses, gleefully sitting around asking how they can make our lives more difficult by trickling out inane updates on their timing and schedule? How could there possibly be that many relevant updates, and to what?

I experienced yet another 22 updates, with another one two days later. They are so arrogant and free from accountability that they do not even feel any obligation to tell us what the updates are for and what impact they may have. What are they anyway, and can we trust them?

If they are so keen on fixing problems and updating things, why do they not fix the problem I have in Word and email where my cursor suddenly jumps from where I am working to somewhere arbitrary on the page?

Why does everyone want my personal information, including my Social Security number, for their data base yet cannot seem to protect it? Three separate data bases in which I am included has been hacked, exposing my private information to who know who. If you cannot protect my information, please do not require it.

You remember Affluenza Teen, referenced in the opening chapter? Well, this spoiled brat, who is apparently sharing a brain cell with his mom, just cannot learn. He was purportedly filmed at a party, drinking, which is a violation of his probation. So, once again, he along with his mother fled to Mexico to avoid any consequences. We the taxpayers had to foot the bill to have the two of them extradited back to the United States to face yet another hearing. Personally, I think the incompetent judge in his first trial should have to foot the bill, just before he is fired for incompetence.

Do you remember Bud, the fifth grader who refused to work and was not held back because his parents would not consent to do so? I later subbed at the middle school and Bud has a replica at the seventh grade level.

*Free Pass*

My guess is that there are hundreds, if not thousands, of Buds.

We have had yet another case of misguided journalistic integrity. Chris Matthews, host of MSNBC's Hardball, had previously committed that he would be "transparent and fair in our coverage" after his wife, Kathleen, announced that she was running as a Democrat for the open seat in Maryland's 8th District. It has since been disclosed that she received a total of $79,050 in campaign contributions from former and current politicians featured on Mr. Matthew's cable news show. As examples: The political action committee for Senator Kirsten Gillibrand (D-NY) gave $10,000 to Mrs. Matthew's campaign two days before she appeared on Hardball. Senator Barbara Boxer (D-Calif.) contributed $1,000 one day before she was interviewed on the show. At least 11 donations came from guests after they appeared on the show. How can anyone in journalism have any shred of integrity, respect and trust when they are able to use their position, status and influence in any but an objective and honest fashion?

We discussed the lack of justice in our justice system, a subject that could easily encompass an entire book. Often times it seems we impose mechanisms, rules and laws to protect honest, hard-working individuals who are victims of circumstances, but then those safeguards end up being used as loopholes by unscrupulous individuals who take advantage of the system and dodge accountability. Case in point: I know a home builder near where I live who purchased a double-wide lake front lot. He then built twin homes priced at over one and one half million dollars each. He moved into one of them as his personal residence and then put the other on the market at the aforementioned price. The real estate bust hit and he could not sell his spec home and ended up negotiating a short sale with the bank. It was one of the very same large banks that accepted bailout money from our tax dollars and then paid huge bonuses to the executives. Short sales happened in thousands of cases across the country and were a saving grace to a lot of good families. In this case though, the builder continued to live in a one plus million dollar lakefront house, had a Porsche in one garage bay, a Mercedes Benz in the next bay and a Hummer in the next, along with two jet skis and a pickup. He still has all of his toys, but has downsized to a top-of-the-line Jeep in place of the Hummer, and he has picked right back up in the building business, I assume with another bank lending him and his ego the funds to do it all over again. Do you think this was the intent of the program?

I have tried my best to avoid naming companies or individuals outright in most cases, but I find myself making an exception in this case. What could we, as the buying public, possibly have done to Liberty Mutual Insurance to bring down the kind of torment, torture and mind-numbing repetition they have chosen to inflict upon us? I addressed the endless parade of commercials on cable television, but Liberty Mutual has chosen to inflict the sort of pain that makes me grab my remote much as a wild west gunfighter would grab his Colt, and instead of firing, I can change the channel in the blink of an eye. There is not just an endless playing of the commercials on multiple channels, but the commercials are an insult to anyone with an intellect. They are obviously done as cheaply as possible, but are also lacking in any semblance of creativity or quality, and we have been subjected to the same ones for a year, and it seems, 100s of times per day. Do you remember the Country Wide Mortgage program commercials a few years ago? I see a lot of similarity. After being beaten up by this company for so long, I have developed such an aversion to them I would never even investigate using them, and I have never had a car named Brad. I almost wish I was insured by them so I could cancel my policy.

Another retailer that requires naming is Staples Office Supply. I purchased an office chair from them less than two years ago. A couple of months ago I noticed that the material on both arms was disintegrating. I went to the Staples where I purchased it, the same one where I purchase(d) all of my office supplies, including printer ink. The manager immediately asked if I purchased the extended plan. I said no, that it had been less than two years and the leather is cracking and falling apart. She replied that their merchandise is only warranted for 14 days. You have to be kidding me. 14 days? Unless of course you want to pay extra for something that is obviously defective. No more purchases from Staples for me.

As a postscript to my comments about cable television and the endless array of channels we have to pay for but do not want, they have now added a new one, the VICE channel. Now that is yet another high class, intellectually stimulating and entertaining channel that I want to pay for. Of course it is also bundled with more worthless channels that I am forced to pay for. Now Comcast, my cable provider, is running a series of commercials that are absolutely laughable. There are two lines that particularly grab my attention. "Our company focus is shifting to customer service." So apparently customer service has not been the focus in the past? "We want to fit into your life." If both of these statements are the case, then I have two questions:

1. Why did it take me working with three different people, including a supervisor, and almost 45 minutes to change my email password recently?

2. Why, if they want to fit into my life, am I unable to choose the channels I want to pay for?

I can recall in high school attending career day and being so impressed with an FBI agent and his presentation that I became enthralled with the idea of joining such an elite and professional organization. At that time they required a degree in either accounting or law, neither of which played to my strengths or interests, so I ended up reluctantly abandoning the idea. Based on what I see going on in today's environment, it is probably just as well. It has become obvious that the director of the FBI and the Attorney General both follow the dictates of the political winds. I could not, in all good conscience, exist and work in an environment so closely dictated by political alliances.

The federal government has grown larger and larger, spending more and more money, and touting that larger is better. But with all of the federal bureaucratic agencies, they cannot seem to track down and deal with the scam robo-call perpetrators, most of them telling me about a credit issue that of course does not exist. We can send men to the moon, we can create incredible computing capacity that we can hold in our hand and we can other amazing things. Why are these scumbags so difficult to track down and deal with? They call from multiple numbers with multiple area codes and multiple city identifiers. Why are they allowed to operate with impunity and with no accountability?

Who is accountable for the food ads on television and in print? Have you ever gone into a fast food restaurant and received a hamburger or taco that actually resembled what you saw in the ad? I got home with a hamburger once and the meat had been left off. That is an extreme case, but what has happened to truth in advertising? Most tacos I get have maybe a tablespoon of meat versus the quarter cup that is shown in the ads.

I live in a tax and spend state, which simply means that the politicians and bureaucrats spend and spend until the well is dry and then raise or add new revenue sources to meet their needs. Oftentimes they get very creative in ways to gouge us so that it flies under the radar of those of us being fleeced. For example, I have a small utility trailer that I use for camping. When it was time to relicense it I received a notice that I needed a new plate, and that there was a fee. My old plate was pristine and I was incredulous. I asked one of my elected representatives why I was required to replace a perfectly good plate. He was honest in his reply; it is for revenue (another word for tax). I do not think my state is much different than the majority of states when it comes to creative ways to bilk us, including what I call phantom taxes. I decided to compile a list of the taxes that I could think of right off the top of my head. Here is my list:

- Federal Income Tax
- State Income Tax (where applicable)
- City and County Income Tax (14 states and DC allow this)
- Property Tax (usually includes school, fire etc.
- Utility Taxes (levied by some cities and municipalities)
- Sales Tax
- Cable and Internet Taxes (take a look at your cable bill, there is a hodgepodge of taxes, and they go up frequently, my cable bill has 10 separate fees, taxes and charges)

*Free Pass*

- Business and Occupation Tax (my state, of course, has this one)
- Cell Phone Taxes (take a look at this bill also and see the myriad of taxes)
- Hotel Taxes (the next time you stay in a hotel look at all of the taxes that are tacked on, according to the city and state)
- Airline Taxes (same thing here, take a look at you itemized bill)
- Rental Car Taxes (another hodgepodge of taxes and fees depending on the city and state) By the way, fees is just another word for taxes.
- Fishing License (license is another word for tax as well) This can involve several different layers of taxes ie. Fresh water, saltwater and shellfish etc. Of course they really sock it to out of state users.
- Hunting License (another opportunity for layering of taxes)
- Federal Duck Stamp (this is the most clever use of an alternative name for a tax: make it into a stamp)
- Real Estate Taxes (in my tax happy state it is an excise tax on the seller of real estate) Nice huh? You get taxed when you sell.
- Driver's License ( not only do they charge you to drive but they punish you with long lines and general incompetence)
- License Plates (Wait, didn't I just pay for a driver's license?)
- Gasoline Taxes (both state and federal- my state has one of the highest state taxes)
- Federal National Park Fee (another tax to use a public site)

- State Park Fee (They call it a Discover Pass in my state) - yea, discover how we can collect more revenue. But this is one of two passes required)
- Vehicle Access Pass (must have to access recreational sites in my state and you must purchase a fishing license to obtain one)
- Professional Licenses (required for most professions in my state and I would guess in most other states - remember a license is just a tax with a tie and sport coat on)
- Corporate License (if you have a corporation you pay this)
- FICA (we all know about this tax)
- Medicare Tax
- Inheritance Tax (excuse me, have taxes of some sort probably not already been paid?)
- Gift Tax
- Alcohol Taxes
- Building Permits (permits are yet another form of taxes)
- Dog License
- Highway Access Fees and Tolls
- Marriage License
- Passport Fee
- Unemployment Taxes
- Self-employment Tax

I am quite sure I have omitted some taxes, licenses and fees, but you get the idea. There is no accountability for creating new ones and increasing existing ones; it is open season on collecting revenue and virtually no mention of cost savings, reducing waste or economizing.

The reality is that it seems that no matter how much tax revenue they raise, they cannot get things right. Two recent examples stand out. The first one is especially scary. It has come to light that the State Of Washington has granted early release to an estimated 3,200 felons, because of a software glitch. Reportedly, this has been going on since 2002. Fourteen years and no one was bright enough or efficient enough to figure it out? Here is the disgraceful part. One early release inmate has been charged with vehicular homicide and another is charged with first-degree murder. They are still looking into how many more crimes may have been committed by the early release prisoners.

The second example of inefficiency, ineffectiveness and wasting of money is not as dangerous as the above example but just shows you what happens when the bureaucracy gets involved in anything. One of the largest in the state and perhaps in all of higher education, IT projects, is estimated at $10 million over budget and at least two years behind schedule.

Since we are on the subject of taxes, I will end this chapter with yet another example of your hard-earned dollars at work. The National Science Foundation spent $412,930 on a scientific paper on the relationship between gender and glaciers. It is quoted as being 10,000-plus words of gobbledygook from a University of Oregon Professor. The study urges scientists to take a feminist political ecology and feminist postcolonial approach when studying melting ice caps and climate change. What better way could you put four hundred thousand dollars to good use?

# Chapter 9 - In Closing
# How Hopeless Is It?

Everyone who has read excerpts from this book as it was being written asked if I had any solutions to the problems and issues I presented. We all know it is much easier to identify problems than it is to come up with solutions. Lack of accountability has caused the problems addressed in this book to become increasingly complex, interrelated, and deeply rooted over time.

While I have been researching, reading the news, and writing this book, I have become increasingly frightened and disheartened. I'm not sure who to trust any more. Those I trusted in the past have betrayed me. Those I thought I could count on have sold out. Those I always thought were objective and fair have turned out to be the total opposite. We are in a major mess and it's getting worse with each passing day. True leadership is a quality in short supply, at a time when we need it the most.

As you have read the chapters you may have said to yourself, "Yes, that is a major problem." Perhaps you experienced frustration, if not anger, but were at a loss when you realized that it is not just a single problem, but a widespread epidemic. The reality is that we have allowed the demise of accountability to occur very gradually over an extended period of time. Loss of accountability has been in stealth mode, aided and abetted by the myriad of bad players involved.

I'm convinced there are other contributing factors. We have groups and sectors of our culture who have worked overtime to convince us they are somehow exempt from any form of accountability. They have been self-inoculated against what they see as the evil virus of accountability. These same groups and individuals have worked with other like-minded individuals to camouflage, hide and deflect their lack of accountability. More often than not they are supported, condoned and championed by politicians, other officials, the entertainment machine, higher education, and the media. After all, they have ordained themselves as the political correctness, cultural and (of course) accountability police. If they say it or ignore it, they must be right. Who are we, the general public, to argue or challenge the omniscient authority of these august individuals?

To conspire is a pretty strong statement, but a lot of these people do tend to scratch each other's backs. Although my optimism has been dampened and my trust and faith in some areas has been torn apart, I still have confidence in the will and determination of the American people. It will take perseverance and a bit of hard work to correct the problems. The first order of business is to get the attention of the offending parties and voice our dissatisfaction.

Why not start with the most egregious offenders, the politicians and appointed officials? As arrogant, self-aggrandizing and seemingly impervious to accountability they may be, they do have some serious chinks in their cloaks of invincibility. There are actually several arrows in our quivers we can use, but a concerted and dedicated effort will be needed. It will require not only our own resolve, but the constant recruitment of others to join the effort. You see, there is one thing greater than the power and influence of the lobbyists: the vote.

The typical politician constantly seeks the golden fleece of reelection. Throughout their term, I believe they focus and concentrate on the lobbyists and their cornucopia of goodies, trinkets and baubles, all exchangeable for votes on key legislation. But closer to crunch time they hone their message to what their constituents want to hear, or at least what they think the voters want to hear, and change their focus to us, at least for that small window we call the election season.

I decided this year that I was going to get more personally involved in the political process and try to make a difference. My new involvement started with my precinct caucus. I found out early on that I would be best served to declare my allegiance to the party, and preferably a particular candidate, assuming I wanted to go forward in the process of selecting a presidential candidate. Somehow I was elected to go to the county convention. There it was reinforced that I was now a certified member of the party and that if I was to have any chance of going to the state convention it would be in my best interest to support a particular candidate. Again, against the odds, I was elected by my peers to go to the state convention.

This is when politics got really interesting. I began to get probing telephone calls and emails as to where my allegiance was going to lie. It was made very clear to me that if I held out any hope of going to the national convention, it would be best if I aligned myself with one particular candidate. I was a bit stunned, and also mystified. This is not how I envisioned the will of the people being served. Instead, the reality seemed to me to be clandestine and contrived. I was particularly outraged that there was no discussion of the qualities necessary for a candidate: namely, the qualities of leadership, character, integrity and values. Yes, there was a platform committee and a presentation of the platform, but I heard no discussion of accountability or its importance. I was expecting serious discussion and debate of the qualifications of all candidates.

My personal concern is that if we keep doing the same things, we are going to continue to get the same results. In the past two elections, and now the current general one, I had no real and viable choice. I am sick and tired of not having a true leader, one with character and values I can trust to lead this country. We need a candidate who truly will provide for and promote the common good. My belief is that this must start with the political parties. Wouldn't it be amazing if the huge group of logical, enlightened and concerned individuals in the middle of the two parties came together and put forth a quality leader? It doesn't hurt to dream.

It is my belief that we will always have a few issues and problems to divide us, which will result in polarization and which we cannot totally agree upon. But I also believe there are a greater number of issues we can agree upon: ones that unite us. I believe most of us want a strong country, one that is prosperous and lives within its means. We want a country that is safe and secure and has a justice system that is fair, consistent and impartial. We long for a media that is also fair, impartial and unbiased, which can be trusted to actually inform us instead of attempting to bend our minds to their agenda, and is a beacon of truth. I believe we all want an educational system that is world class and a role model for excellence. We want an entertainment and sports industry that recognizes the social, cultural and ethical responsibilities and humbles themselves to what their real roles are … to entertain and amuse us. I believe we want corporations to be good corporate citizens, to be honest and forthright, demonstrating character, and treating customers and employees like they really matter. Above all else, I think we all want those we elect to be good stewards to all the people they serve, not some select few. In short, I strongly believe we all want accountability.

As I suggest some things we might consider doing to reverse this trend of diminishing accountability, I want to emphasize one thing. They are steps I have taken personally, and what anyone else chooses to do depends on their own personal level of concern and the choices they wish to make. I would hope that people discuss, contemplate and then come up with even more creative ways to promote accountability and for it to become a priority. It will require involvement and commitment.

There are so many big issues in this country at the current time to occupy everyone; it is understandable that some things inevitably take a back seat. There are the issues of the economy, of security, immigration and the general dysfunctionality in Washington. It is easy to forget about the waste, and the influence of special interests and lobbyists. We tend to overlook the politicizing of the courts, the Justice Department and the FBI. We get so locked onto political agendas and ideologies we forget about character, integrity and what is good for the country. We have become so conditioned by political rhetoric that we only have vague memories of what leadership looks like and how leaders are supposed to behave.

*Free Pass*

It is my belief that we can fix the economy, stabilize and normalize immigration, and fix the dysfunctionality in Washington, while at the same time imposing term limits, cleaning up waste, imposing campaign spending reform, limiting access and influence of lobbyists, eliminating lifetime appointments of judges, including the Supreme Court, and decoupling politics, as much as possible, from the DOJ and the FBI. How you choose to become proactive in the reform process and reinstitution of accountability is up to you. It can be as simple as being a more informed and discerning voter. It can be by becoming a dedicated letter writer and emailer to candidates and elected officials. It can be by getting involved in the political process and attending meetings and candidate forums. It can be by writing letters to the editors of relevant publications. You can also take this as an opportunity to express your demands that you want a factual, unbiased and objective press and media. Can you imagine the impact that thousands upon thousands of letters and emails would have on elected officials, corporate CEOs, entertainers, school superintendents, college presidents and deans, judges and media moguls?

If you have a child in college, especially a public college or university, tell the president and deans that you expect your child to be only exposed to the relevant academic subject matter, not the professors' spiritual, political or cultural views. You are paying for an academic education and job skills, not an indoctrination into someone's philosophy or beliefs.

Get involved with your local school district by making it known that you expect good performance from all teachers, and that none are exempt from performance expectations. Send this same message to your legislators and state superintendents.

You might also write to your state elected officials stating the same concerns and expectations regarding indoctrinations by professors. You might also address the issue of tenure at the same time. Tenure is nothing more than a free pass to ignore accountability. No one should have a guaranteed lifetime job, especially one funded by tax dollars. If it is the position of the state to pass out lifetime jobs, where does the line form?

I choose where I shop and where I spend my money based on several factors. First, I do not want to be subjected to any political or cultural ideologies or agendas. Secondly, I want them to be at least somewhat accountable as demonstrated by their customer service, their honesty and forthrightness and responsiveness. I know that my choice to not patronize a company such as Starbucks, has virtually no impact on them, but it gives me a great deal of satisfaction knowing I have walked the walk regarding accountability and the arrogance of big corporations. Besides, I have saved a great deal of money at the same time and have not gone into caffeine withdrawal. It is a rewarding side benefit to realize I am saving over $100 per month on coffee. If enough people decide to take a stand and say enough is enough, I believe the voice of accountability will be heard. There is power in numbers.

As for the entertainment industry, I have chosen to pretty much avoid going to the movies and watching certain television programs. I am fed up with helping fund an industry with no accountability, a de facto political fund-raising organization and an insult to intelligence and good character. I am not going to pad the pockets of a bunch of arrogant and self-centered entertainers and entertainment executives whose mission is to corrupt and negatively influence our youth, while at the same time trying to influence politics, cultural and social values and assuming the role of monitors of political correctness. There is no other group who works on self-aggrandizement more than the entertainment and sports industry. I certainly pay no attention to the late night entertainers (humorists) and their slanted and self-promoting agendas. Do you ever see or hear them being critical or making jokes about their own corrupt industry?

I pretty much discount the media as a source of honest and factual information these days. I try to ferret out, as best I can, information sources I can trust and rely on. I scrutinize the credibility and credentials of the source. I try to look at multiple sources and really dig for the truth, although it is becoming increasingly difficult to find. If the media was a court, an innocent man would not stand a chance: sensationalism sells. If we ever needed a media probing for and ferreting out the truth, it is now. We need a media who is a watchdog for honesty, values and transparency. Someone who holds wrongdoers accountable.

I honestly do not have an approach to some of the most arrogant and blatant offenders of corporate accountability: Microsoft and Apple. After all, they have created somewhat of a unique dual monopoly. If there was a viable alternative I would be all over it. Their hubris and arrogance sets the standard when it comes to a lack of accountability.

Likewise, I am waiting for something to replace the cable company that is affordable, gives you freedom of choice, and has customer service as a core component and value. Call me crazy, but I am sick of being forced by a virtual monopoly to pay for things I do not want or use, all the while enduring terrible customer service. So far the single biggest chink I have found in the cable company's armor of no accountability is the Federal Communications Commission. I recently had a billing issue I could not resolve with Comcast, so I went on line and filed a complaint with the FCC. A few days later I received a call from Comcast asking to resolve the issue. I will also pound on my elected officials about the absurd practice of bundling channels. Why is it even necessary to have to spend extraordinary amounts of time and effort for something that should be a given? My local electric company is somewhat regulated at the state and local level; why are the cable companies not regulated? Cable is a golden letter-writing opportunity.

Perhaps you are not concerned about accountability. Perhaps it is an item very low on your list of priorities. Maybe you see it as a hopeless situation and one which you can have little if any control over. In that case you still have the freedom to do nothing, while Rome, I mean Washington, continues to burn. As for me, I am fed up, so I wrote a book and will take every opportunity to confront the problem and take whatever action I can. Trust me, elected officials, the media and the entertainment industry have us right where they want us: complacent, helpless and frustrated. I have never been a complacent person and I am frustrated. I believe in confronting problems and seeking solutions. I hope we can start a dialogue and begin to demand accountability. I really want to trust again. Trust and accountability are inextricably tied together. I want to feel that I have advocates in politics, in the media and in the justice system. I want to see honesty, integrity, responsibility and character as givens once more.

I began this book by saying I am mad and frightened. By the end of this book, after reading and watching what is going on and connecting the dots, I am horrified and saddened. I sometimes feel like the voice crying in the wilderness. I hope we're not too late.

*To my readers:*

*Thank you for reading my book. Please write a review and tell your friends about this book. I appreciate each and every one of you.*

*M. Randall Long*

# *About the Author*

Born and raised in Texas, M. Randall Long has lived in the Pacific Northwest since 1992. He served as a survival instructor for the United States Air Force during the Vietnam war, and then worked in the corporate world for most of his career.

His work experience includes the oil and gas business, high-tech and bio-tech, and retail. He has also taught college classes as an adjunct, and has travelled extensively in the United States and overseas.

Long loves anything in the outdoors, and still loves to travel. He is currently involved in numerous community endeavors.

In the past couple of years, he was inspired to write about his observations on world and national affairs, and belongs to an author critique group in his hometown. *Free Pass* is his first book.

48389015R00081

Made in the USA
San Bernardino, CA
24 April 2017